D1553227

PROOF
of LIFE *after* LIFE

PROOF
of LIFE after LIFE

7 Reasons to Believe
There Is an Afterlife

RAYMOND A. MOODY, MD
author of the bestseller *Life After Life*

and PAUL PERRY
coauthor of the bestseller *Evidence of the Afterlife*

ATRIA BOOKS
New York London Toronto Sydney New Delhi

 BEYOND WORDS
Portland, Oregon

ATRIA BOOKS
An Imprint of Simon & Schuster, Inc.
1230 Avenue of the Americas
New York, NY 10020

BEYOND WORDS
1750 S.W. Skyline Blvd., Suite 20
Portland, Oregon 97221-2543
503-531-8700 / 503-531-8773 fax
www.beyondword.com

Managing editor: Lindsay Easterbrooks-Brown
Editor: Michele Ashtiani Cohn & Bailey Potter
Copyeditor: Kristin Thiel, Emmalisa Sparrow Wood
Proofreader: Ashley Van Winkle
Design: Devon Smith
Composition: William H. Brunson Typography Services

First Beyond Words/Atria Books hardcover edition September 2023

ATRIA BOOKS and colophon are trademarks of Simon & Schuster, Inc.
BEYOND WORDS PUBLISHING is an imprint of Simon & Schuster, Inc., and the Beyond Words logo is a registered trademark of Beyond Words Publishing, Inc.

For more information about special discounts for bulk purchases, please contact Simon & Schuster Special Sales at 1-866-506-1949 or business@simonandschuster.com.

The Simon & Schuster Speakers Bureau can bring authors to your live event.
For more information or to book an event, contact the Simon & Schuster Speakers Bureau at 1-866-248-3049 or visit our website at www.simonspeakers.com.

Manufactured in the United States of America

10 9 8 7 6 5 4 3 2 1

Library of Congress Control Number: 2023938097

ISBN: 978-1-58270-920-8
ISBN: 978-1-66801-071-6 (eBook)

The corporate mission of Beyond Words Publishing, Inc.: *Inspire to Integrity*

Dedicated with love to my wife, Cheryl, and the children in our lives, Carter, Carol, Avery, Samuel, and Ray Junior.

—Raymond A. Moody, MD, PhD

To my wife, Darlene, and the children and grandchildren who make our world.

—Paul Perry

Contents

Foreword

———————— ✳ ————————

Humanity received a tremendous gift when Dr. Raymond Moody
published his world-changing book *Life After Life*, in 1975. As
a professor of philosophy fascinated by the ancient Greeks, he was
inspired by such brilliant minds as Plato who documented human
reports suggestive of life after death.

It was a series of remarkable stories from over 100 patients who
shared their experiences of almost dying that led Professor Moody to
publish his research, providing an intriguing glimpse into the modern
reality of an afterlife suggested by those early Greek philosophers. And
yet, he realized that these were by their very nature subjective reports
by the dying themselves, and what the rational world would ultimately
require would be some confirmatory body of quantifiable, objective
evidence.

Although he has written several books over the ensuing decades
that are directly relevant to the afterlife question, the book you are holding is his first direct effort at consolidating numerous overlapping lines
of evidence to bolster the objective support of the reality of the afterlife.

Millions around the world are aware of Dr. Moody's contributions as
the father of the field by coining the term *near-death experiences* (NDEs)
in 1975, but far fewer are aware of his remarkable book *Glimpses of
Eternity*, published in 2010. This work was entirely devoted to shared
death experiences, which consist of many of the same extraordinary
ingredients of the NDE but occur in normal, healthy bystanders, either
at the bedside of or at some distance from a person who is dying.

In the current work, he expands greatly on the concept of the shared
death experience, elaborating the myriad ways in which they offer

objective proof to claims of consciousness beyond the confines of the brain and body, and confirms our notions of soul and of the ability of loving relationships to exist beyond the death of a physical body.

This expansion incorporates major new fields of work in afterlife studies, such as modern documentation of out-of-body experiences and precognitive experiences involving spiritual events (including some deeply personal to Dr. Moody and his family and friends). In addition, he discusses terminal (or paradoxical) lucidity, the apparent brief coming back to life with full cognitive, emotional, and communicative skills of people thought to have irreversible brain damage that would not have allowed such lucidity, and yet these cases are not uncommon.

He discusses specific cases of the transformative power of light, as well as inexplicable healing and new abilities enabled by near-death experiences. Especially fascinating are the details he shares of his use of the psychomanteum, an ancient Greek technique of mirror gazing that he has found remarkably effective in opening doors of communication with departed loved ones.

All in all, this book provides a rich compendium of case reports and comprehensive analysis to allow Dr. Moody to offer a career-summarizing work that fully supports and brings to fruition the promise of his 1975 book *Life After Life*. This book does indeed provide robust proof of life after life! Enjoy!

—**Eben Alexander, MD**, former Harvard neurosurgeon
and author of *Proof of Heaven, The Map of Heaven,*
and *Living in a Mindful Universe*

Preface

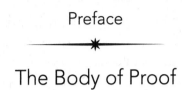

The Body of Proof

It was 1987 when my literary agent, Nat Sobel, asked me to coauthor a book with Dr. Raymond Moody. That presented a problem for me. Despite being the executive editor of *American Health* magazine, a flourishing general health publication, I had no idea of who Raymond Moody was, let alone what a near-death experience (NDE) was all about.

My agent was shocked when he heard that. "Haven't you ever heard of *Life After Life?*" he asked. "Don't you ever watch *Oprah?*"

We were halfway through lunch, and my lack of knowledge about Dr. Moody and his field of study cast a silence over the table. I felt, well, ignorant.

Nat changed the subject, and I thought discussion of Dr. Moody's unwritten book had evaporated. But it hadn't. Nat finished his burger and dropped a note from his jacket pocket into the middle of the table.

"Here's Moody's phone number; give him a call," he said. "You need to know this guy and this subject. It'll be an education."

I called Dr. Moody that night and found him to be relaxed and friendly, not the stiff doctor I had expected. He told me to call him Raymond and was actually thrilled to discover that I had never heard of him and knew nothing about near-death experiences. "We can start with a blank slate," he said. The next week I flew to see him in Georgia, and he picked me up from the airport. He lived more than an hour west of the airport, which gave us a chance to talk about a wide variety of subjects: buried gold; criminal behavior (Raymond is a psychiatrist, after all); politics; and, oh yes, near-death experiences (NDEs). By the time we arrived at his home, I had agreed to cowrite what would become our first book. The subject was new and fascinating to me, and while writing *The Light Beyond*, I learned the basics of what makes up an NDE: that many who almost die leave their body during that time, that they often see departed loved ones, and that most are exposed to a light that emanates kindness and wisdom. I was hooked. I decided then and there to devote myself to creating a library of wisdom dedicated to Raymond and his expertise in the field of NDEs.

To a great extent, that library has now been accomplished. Counting *Proof of Life after Life*, we have now coauthored six books, along with creating two films and maintaining an audio collection of several hundred interviews. These recordings are truly special, combining the rush of the creek passing by Raymond's home in rural Alabama and the rolling sound of his rocking chair to make his impromptu lectures that much more hypnotic. Every time I listen to one of these recordings, I am projected back to the day of the interview and the feeling of gratitude I had at being there.

What astounds me when I listen to these recordings is the profound change Raymond has made in his own belief of an afterlife. When we first began working together, he shunned the idea that near-death experiences are proof of an afterlife. His reasoning for skepticism was clear: NDEs are subjective experiences that can only be perceived by the person who has them. So, to present proof of such a bold belief as consciousness surviving bodily death, the event itself would have to be witnessed by at least one other person. And I don't mean watching somebody as they die but in some way objectively joining them in their actual death experience. This type of witness is called a shared death experience (SDE), which, as you will see in this book, is when a living person somehow participates in the events of a dying person.

SDEs come in a variety of forms: seeing mist leave a person's dying body is one such form; communicating psychically with a dying person from a distance would be another; and so on.

Raymond and I began earnestly researching SDEs around the year 2005, but we had been aware of them for more than a decade prior, reading about events that had happened hundreds of years earlier and listening to contemporary ones. We even mentioned them in our first book, including some very descriptive SDEs that are included in this book as well. Then one day in our rocking chairs it came to us: SDEs *are proof* of an afterlife. That sudden realization shifted our research to collecting and studying SDEs, organizing them into categories.

We feel the information collected within these pages proves that consciousness survives bodily death. To go a step further, Raymond feels the mass of objective evidence afforded by SDEs means that it is no longer necessary to prove an afterlife—rather, disbelievers should have to prove there isn't an afterlife.

"For people to anticipate life after death is a fully rational thing to do," says Raymond. "I can't think of any way around the evidence. I've tried but I can't. So I say, yes, belief in life after death is rational."

The pages ahead contain the body of that rational proof.

—**Paul Perry**

Introduction

✳

Beyond Near-Death Experiences

No one knows whether death is really the greatest blessing a man can have, but they fear it is the greatest curse, as if they knew well.

—Plato

It's hard to imagine that the near-death experience (NDE) by itself doesn't represent proof positive of life after death.

I am not a doubter of NDEs. After all, I named and defined the near-death experience in 1975.[1] I personally believe NDEs to be partial evidence of an afterlife. I have listened to enough people tell of leaving their bodies, seeing dead relatives, and witnessing a bright and intelligent light that I have come to agree with William James, the nineteenth-century psychologist and philosopher whose own NDE led him to say: "He sees, but cannot define the light which bathes him and by means of which he sees the objects which excite his wonder. If we cannot explain physical light, how can we explain the light which is the truth itself? . . . But do you wish, Lord, that I should inclose [sic] in poor and barren words sentiments which the heart alone can understand?"[2]

Still, when I completed my initial NDE research for *Life After Life*, I realized that my work still did not answer the question of many readers, the one that Plato considered to be the most important question in the world: *What happens when we die?*

The NDE itself is a subjective event that is not experienced by any but the single person who has it. And although NDE stories alone might be considered proof of an afterlife by many, it's the subjective nature of the experience that would keep it from standing up in court as proof positive of an afterlife. In other words, it's difficult to believe a near-death experience and the afterlife it portends, until you have had one.

Limits of the NDE

I believe NDEs to be true evidence of the afterlife, but I know, too, that they are subjective events, without objective proof, leaving myself and other believers to speak with a subjective heart and not an objective brain.

In my early research, I was interpreting my own material with objective intent—I was analyzing an interesting medical phenomenon and felt a sense of scientific duty in naming and defining it. After speaking to so many enthusiastic experiencers, I felt in my subjective heart there was life after life, but my objectivity didn't go beyond intent; I didn't have solid proof that would stand up to what I myself had been taught in graduate school. And anyway, I am not comfortable telling people what to believe, especially about such an important topic. So, I kept my opinion to myself and let readers make up their own minds based on the "evidence" I could provide.

I examined all the case studies I had compiled, and in the summer of 1975, I derived fourteen common traits that summarized what I came to name the near-death experience, or NDE.

1. **Ineffability:** These experiences have been virtually inexpressible because there are no words in our community of language to express consciousness at the point of death. In fact, many people who've had NDEs say things like "There are just no words to express what I am trying to say." This presents a problem, of course, because if someone can't describe what's happened, they can't give to or gain from another person an understanding of their NDE.

2. **Hearing the Death Pronouncement:** Numerous people in the course of my research told of hearing their doctors or others pronounce them dead.

3. **Feelings of Peace and Quiet:** Many people described pleasant feelings and sensations during their experience, even after being pronounced dead. One man with a severe head injury and no detectable vital signs said that all pain vanished as he floated in a dark space and realized "I must be dead."

4. **Noise:** In many of the cases, people reported unusual auditory sensations, like a loud buzzing noise or a loud ring. Some found this noise to be quite pleasant while others found it to be extremely annoying.

5. **A Dark Tunnel:** People reported the sensation of being pulled rapidly through a dark space, most often described as a tunnel. For instance, a man who died during burns and fall injuries said that he escaped into a "dark void" in which he floated and tumbled through space.

6. **Out-of-Body:** During these experiences, usually after the tunnel experience, most people had the sense of leaving their body and looking at themselves from a physical point outside of it. Some described it as being "the third person in the room" or like being "on stage in a play." The experiences they had out-of-body were quite detailed. Many of the people described medical procedures and activity with such detail that there was little doubt on the part of attending physicians interviewed later that the usually comatose patient had actually witnessed events that happened during the NDE.

7. **Meeting Others:** Out-of-body experiences were then often followed by the meeting of other "spiritual beings" in their vicinity, beings who were there to ease them through the transition and into death or to tell them that it wasn't their time to die.

8. **A Being of Light:** The most incredible common element I found and the one with the greatest effect on the individual was the

encounter with a very bright light, one that was most often described as a "being of light." Time and again in the accounts, this being first appeared as a dim light and then became rapidly brighter until it reached an unearthly brilliance. Often described as "Jesus," "God," or an "angel" by those with religious training, the light communicated with the individual (sometimes in a language they had never even heard), often asking them if they were "ready to die" or what their accomplishments were. The being of light did not ask these questions in a judgmental way. Rather it asked Socratic questions, ones aimed at acquiring information that could help the person proceed along a path of truth and self-realization.

9. **A Review:** The probing questions by the being of light often led to a review of one's life, a moment of startling power during which a person's entire life was displayed before them in panoramic intensity. The review was extraordinarily rapid and in chronological order, incredibly vivid and real. Sometimes it was even described as "three-dimensional." Others describe it as "highly charged" with emotions and even multiple dimensions in a way that the individual could understand the thoughts of everyone in the review.

10. **A Border or Limit:** In some of these cases, the person described approaching a "border" or "limit" beyond which they would not return. This border was described variously as being water, a gray mist, a door, a fence across a field, or even a line or an imaginary line. In one case, the person was escorted to the line by the being of light and asked if he wanted to die. When he said he knew nothing about death, the being told him, "Come over this line, and you will learn." When he did, he experienced "the most wonderful feeling" of peace and tranquility and a vanishing of all worries.

11. **Coming Back:** Obviously, the individuals I've interviewed came back to their physical lives. Some resisted their return and wanted

to stay in this afterlife state. Some reported return trips through the tunnel and back to their physical bodies. But when they did return, they had moods and positive feelings that lingered for a long time. Many were so positively transformed that their pre-NDE personalities disappeared, and they became almost unrecognizable from their old selves.

12. **Not Telling Others:** The people I spoke with were normal, with functioning, well-balanced personalities. Yet because they were afraid of being labeled as delusional or mentally ill, these people often chose to remain silent about their experience or only related it to someone very close to them. Because there was no common language in which to express their experience, they chose to keep it to themselves so no one would think they had become mentally unbalanced as a result of their brush with death. It wasn't until many individuals heard of the research I was doing that they felt comfortable enough to relate their experience to others. I was frequently thanked by these long-silent near-death experiencers (NDErs), who would say things like, "Thank you for your work. Now I know I'm not crazy."

13. **Positive Effects on Life:** Despite the desire of most of these individuals to remain quiet about their experiences, the effect of these experiences on their lives was profound and noticeable. Many told me their lives had broadened and deepened through these experiences, that they had become more reflective of life and gentler with those around them. Their vision left them with new goals, new moral principles, and a renewed determination to live in accordance with them.

14. **New Views of Death:** They all reported new views about death. They no longer feared death, yet many had the sense that they had a lot of personal growth to attend to before leaving their physical

lives. They also came to believe that there was no "reward and punishment" model of the afterlife. Rather, the being of light made their "sinful" deeds obvious to them and made it clear that life was a learning process, not a platform for later judgment.

Developing these common traits was the most important aspect of my research and—when I think about it—probably the most important thing I will do in my entire life. Before, no one had ever truly studied these experiences, despite every single element of the NDE being present throughout recorded human history. It was all right there in plain sight, yet no one had pulled it all together and made it digestible for the public.

The work I did in writing *Life After Life* opened the door to a large amount of medical and philosophical research on the subject of death, information that was greatly needed by those who'd had one of these puzzling experiences and could now take comfort in the knowledge that they were not alone.

However, many who read this book took it further. They believed I had cracked the code and had finally proven life after death. That most certainly wasn't the case. As amazing as these common traits are, they lack one thing—objectivity.

An Understandable Conclusion

I can understand why people confuse NDEs with proof of an afterlife. In just reading the traits I suggested, I can recognize that they contain many of the elements of the afterlife discussed in almost all religions. But these NDE elements also brought up many sticky questions about NDEs themselves, namely about their subjectivity and how far such subjectivity could go in proving anything but one's hopeful dying dream. I realized that to connect NDEs and life after death would require further research, and I wasn't sure that was a direction I even wanted to take.

For one thing, I rarely involved myself in such speculation. From the very beginning of my NDE research until now, I have made it clear that NDEs are subjective and not scientific proof of much more than observation of the NDEr themselves. But I also think it's fair to let people draw their own conclusions. And let's face it, telling people about a person who experiences clinical death, leaves their body, sees dead relatives, and encounters a loving being of light can certainly set the mind afire.

Hints of Shared Death Experiences

It has long been rumored that I was ostracized by my professors at the Medical College of Georgia for writing such a "weird" book. That never was the case. Rather, they supported me and my work with deep interest. It was unusual for a week to go by that I didn't have two or three doctors asking if they could listen to my taped audio interviews of those who were opening up about their death experiences. Those curious doctors almost always heard in these stories events that had taken place with their own patients or even themselves, most of which fit into the mold of those in my book.

I also learned from my colleagues that the stories these patients told them also included those that did not fit into the standard definition of NDEs. In fact, they didn't fit anywhere that I was familiar with. The events they talked about were similar to NDEs, only they had happened not to the sick or dying but to people who were bystanders to a person's dying experience. For example, some of these patients reported the presence of deceased family members who appeared at the deathbed to help the dying loved one complete their passage. Others heard ethereal music as their loved ones died. Rarely was only one bystander at the bedside when these phenomena took place. Rather, there were at least two in the room and at other times an entire family, all of whom reported witnessing the same supernatural experience.

A Parallel Experience

The death-related stories I was hearing from patients contained objective elements that seemed linked to NDEs but were not NDEs. They were instead a different category, one in which a person's death experience was somehow conveyed to a bystander who would then experience it.

These shared events did not always take place at the deathbed. Some of these took place at a distance from the dying person, some even halfway around the world. Many took place in the form of accurate dreams or visions foretelling the death of a loved one.

I also discovered many of these experiences while conducting historical medical research. For instance, I found a trove of these types of experiences while exploring the archives of the nineteenth-century research of the founders of the Society for Psychical Research (SPR) in England. A two-volume opus published by the SPR was *Phantasms of the Living*, compiled by pioneering researchers Edmund Gurney, Frederic W. H. Myers, and Frank Podmore and contained more than seven hundred cases regarding paranormal phenomena, many of these deathbed visions and other forms of what I would soon call shared death experiences (SDEs). Although none of the men were formally trained in research, their techniques for gathering and fact-checking were impeccable. The three went to great lengths to communicate with more than one person about each of the collected case studies.

Another book, *Death-Bed Visions: The Psychical Experiences of the Dying*, contained the work of Sir William Barrett, a physics professor at the Royal College of Science in Dublin. Though it was not published until 1926, after Barrett's death, it was nothing less than the first scientific study of the minds of the dying. He concluded, among other important information, that dying patients are often clear thinking and rational and the events around them are often spiritual and supernatural.

A New Mold for Death Experiences

Many of the experiences collected by these early researchers fit neatly into a similar mold and were told by loved ones who spent a significant amount of time caring for the dying. I realized that these empathic experiences belonged in a category of their own because they were experiences of dying that could be subjectively shared with the living.

I didn't seek out stories of these SDEs at the time because I was still collecting more and more NDE accounts. Instead, I filed these stories in some of my many notebooks where I record future projects. Eventually I came to call them SDEs because that term was broad enough to encompass all that they were: occurrences where a person who is alive and well shares the death experience of a person who is dying.

An SDE of My Own

It's at this point that I want to reveal a personal case study. My long-time readers may have heard this story before, but it bears repeating because this SDE opened my eyes to a new field of afterlife study.

Nineteen years after beginning to think about SDEs, I had one. I should say, my whole adult family had one.

Our mother, at the age of seventy-four, received a diagnosis of non-Hodgkin's lymphoma. This cancer of the white blood cells had progressed so far by the time the doctor recognized the disease that the doctor said chemotherapy would have little effect, and she had less than two weeks to live.

Mom had been the pillar of our family, and now we needed to be her pillar. We all gathered in Macon, Georgia, where she lived and was now hospitalized, to be with her during her final days. There were six of us—siblings and in-laws—and we all worked hard to provide her with as much comfort and love as we possibly could. We cared for her only a few days at home before she became too sick for that; we all moved to the hospital to make sure she wouldn't be alone.

On what would be her last day, we were again all gathered in her room. There was my wife, Cheryl, and me; my police officer brother and his wife; and our sister and her husband, a minister. Mom had been comatose for the last two days, but now she awoke and tried to speak to us through her oxygen mask.

"Please say that again," said my sister, Kay.

Batting the oxygen mask from her face, she said with a weak voice, "I love you all very much."

Her moment of lucidity gave us hope that she would make it another day or two. But a few minutes after her declaration of love, she waned so severely that it became obvious that the end was minutes away.

We all held hands in a circle around her bed and waited for her to pass. As we did, the room suddenly changed shape—for all of us. For me, it became the shape of an hourglass. Four of the six of us felt as though we were being lifted off the ground in a glass elevator. I felt a strong pull upward, as did two of the other five.

"Look," said my sister, pointing toward the end of the bed. "Dad's here! He's come back to get her!"

Several of us saw him. And when I say, "saw him," I mean we saw him as solid as though he were standing in front of us in the flesh.

Everyone reported that the light in the room had acquired a soft and fuzzy texture and was opaque like the light in a swimming pool at night.

These mystical events were not frightening. Rather, they seemed to be communication from another world that caused sadness to leave the room and be replaced with great joy. My brother-in-law, a Methodist minister, summed it up for all of us when he said, "I felt like I left my physical body and went into another plane with her. It was like nothing that has ever happened to me."

After Mom died, we spent the next few days tying up the loose ends that are always left after a death. During that time, we all compared notes and concluded that what should have been one of the least happy days of our lives was actually one of our most joyous. We all agreed that we had traveled at least partway to heaven with our mother and—with the visitation of our father—had shared a number of her death experiences on the way. It was the only conclusion we could reach.[3]

Proving There's an Afterlife

In addition to my personal SDE story, I've nearly died twice in my life. I am no longer afraid of death, knowing what I've come to believe through my research as well as my own experiences. But belief is not enough to convince others. This brings us to how I can convince you of the proof of an afterlife.

As a philosophy professor, I've taught numerous university courses on the question of postmortem consciousness survival. My courses did not focus on arguments that support the possibility of an afterlife. The course content always focused on the objections and difficulties that great thinkers identified and eloquently articulated.

It is pointless to go on about this important investigation while looking for reasons that support or favor there being an afterlife. C. S. Lewis once said, "If you look for truth, you may find comfort in the end: if you look for comfort you will not get either comfort or truth —only soft soap and wishful thinking to begin with and, in the end, despair."[4]

Therefore, intellectual honesty and simple kindness to our fellow human beings demand that we formulate the notion of proof of an afterlife precisely and consciously. What is *proof* anyway? *Proof* is a rational means of leading everyone who follows it to the same logical conclusion. But a whole spectrum of varying meanings has become attached to the word. So, we need to get specific.

Regrettably, *proof* is a conspicuous word often seen on tabloid headlines that smacks of sensationalism and fires up emotions. Obviously, we will avoid the sensational or undesired use of the word since life after death is a topic that affects vulnerable people's feelings. We need to

delineate the kind of proof to which life after death might be suscepti-
ble very carefully.

So, how can I prove there is an afterlife while being mindful of the
gravity of the word and people's emotions and beliefs? Just as I did with
the NDE—by telling real people's stories, as well as exploring my fellow
researchers' experiences and studies, categorizing them into clear reasons, which each add weight to the conclusion.

Stories Tell the Story

All of this—the initiation of my journey into the study of afterlife
research, the realization that the presence of SDEs could be the missing link of objectivity to proving the existence of an afterlife, and my
increasing collection of stories of SDEs from people around the world
and my own personal experiences—has led to my goal of proving the
existence of an afterlife.

So, *Proof of Life after Life* is a book that presents the new arena
for death studies, one that focuses on the nature of consciousness and
explores the certainty that consciousness separates from the body at the
point of death. Does consciousness arise out of neuronal material
(the brain), and is it able to exist separate from brain matter, especially
at times of high stress like death? If so, does consciousness, separate
from the brain, amount to the soul? And does that soul depart for a new
plane of existence?

Perhaps these questions can be answered through the collection
of more objective information, which is the goal in studying SDEs. In
this book, you'll find a wide variety of stories that each help tell the
greater story of *Proof of Life after Life*, a few of which you may recognize from my other books—I consider these my "greatest hits"—while
others have been published in other afterlife researchers' books, from the
eighteenth century to the present. One of the reasons for the wide range
of accounts from over the years is because a report from two hundred
years ago contains the same elements as a modern record—it shows that

the stories were worth noting even then for their peculiarity. And now, to honor the people whom these stories belong to and the researchers over the centuries who have collected the stories, they get to support my proof that consciousness survives bodily death.

1

Shared Death Experiences

There are only two ways to live your life. One is as though nothing is a miracle. The other is as though everything is a miracle.

—Albert Einstein

With my mother's death, I now knew what it was like to have a shared death experience (SDE). I also knew that the experience was real because the same events that happened to me were reported by the other five stable bystanders.

I felt oddly elevated by this experience, as though I were now on the high road that I always knew was there but had yet to see for myself. It reminded me of something a man said to me when recounting his near-death experience (NDE). "No one really believes these experiences until they have one," he said, "then they become true believers and can't talk about anything else."

And that was how it became for me. The sense of having shared my mother's death was convincing proof of so much I had studied and assumed about death experiences. Now I had been present for a case that contained objective proof. I could easily have left the field of death studies right there and been satisfied that I had seen proof of a living soul in an SDE. What more was there left to research?

Quite a bit, actually.

I wanted to hear more stories of SDEs from firsthand experiencers, and as a result, I began to solicit them at every opportunity. The content of my lectures changed. Now I spiced my talks with questions to the audience about SDEs. To do this, I included the story of my mother's death followed by my definition of the SDE: "A shared death experience can consist of some of the same elements that we use to define a near-death experience. But the difference is that the person to whom the experience occurs is not themselves near death. Nor are they ill or injured. Rather they are in the presence of somebody who is dying. And as they observe the other person's dying process, they co-live that person's dying experience so closely that I have come to call these experiences empathic."

I would then ask how many in the audience had had such an experience. As many as one in fifteen usually raised their hands. After I told them my mother's story and they had a deeper understanding of the experience, I asked again how many had had such an experience. The number changed substantially, with about three in fifteen raising their hands. This astounded me, because it was almost the same number who raised their hands when asked if they'd had a near-death experience (NDE).

I was excited at the notion of researching unexplored territory. As had been the case with my early studies of the NDE, there was virtually no modern medical research dealing with SDEs. When they were discussed at all, it was generally as an artifact to an NDE. In essence, SDEs were a topic with no name, sometimes discussed but barely explored. The few researchers who did mention them seemed to realize what gold they had: SDEs might be objective proof of the soul separating from the body, proof of telepathy, evidence of a shared memory. It was all there in that one experience.

As a student of philosophy as well, I found myself carried by this new area of study back to the ancient Greeks. The afterlife was of great interest to the Greek philosophers. Socrates called the study of the afterlife "care of the soul,"[1] and therefore one of the most important things a person could do.

So important is the study of the afterlife that Socrates, on his deathbed, was reported to have said to his friend Cimmias that:

although it is very difficult if not impossible in this life to achieve certainty about these questions, at the same time it is utterly feeble not to use every effort in testing the available theories, or to leave off before we have considered them in every way, and come to the end of our resources. It is our duty to do one of two things, either to ascertain the facts, whether by seeking instruction or by personal discovery, or, if this is impossible, to select the best and most dependable theory which human intelligence can supply.[2]

Guidance of Plato

The approach I took in studying SDEs was the same used by Plato, who believed that studying individual experiences was the key to researching the afterlife. Without these experiences, he felt there was little to guide the way.

Plato took seriously the importance of the search for the afterlife. In *Phaedo*, Socrates defines death as a "separation of the soul from the body" and is thrilled that his death will come soon, which it does, given that he had just been poisoned and is on his deathbed as he speaks.[3]

Plato derived through observation that the study of stories is the only true way to explore proof of the afterlife. It is from his persistent examination of case studies that he could summarize this philosophy toward death: "Either death is a state of nothingness and utter unconsciousness, or, as men say, there is a change and migration of the soul from this world to another. . . . Now if death be of such a nature, I say that to die is [to] gain; for eternity is then only a single night."[4]

I agree with Plato's genius, as least when it comes to the value of case studies. It is by examining case studies that I, too, conduct my research, because without them, there would be little to guide the way.

It is through the collection and examination of case studies regarding different types of SDEs that I have been able to determine several objective reasons to believe in the afterlife.

Beyond the NDE

Much modern-day research into the subject of the afterlife seems to begin and end with the near-death experience. Maybe it should begin with the NDE, but it should not end there. Although NDEs are profound experiences that contain all the elements one would expect of a deeply mystical experience (as many perceive death to be), the NDE is a subjective experience that happens to one person and cannot be experienced by anyone but the person who actually has it.

It is the subjective nature of NDEs that make them circumstantial evidence and therefore do not provide proof beyond a reasonable doubt, which is what we are seeking.

SDEs, however, do provide proof beyond reasonable doubt that the soul survives bodily death. By definition they are experiences in which one or more person(s) share in a dying person's transition.

For example, several people attending the deathbed of an individual may report seeing an apparition visit the dying person. They may not know who the apparition was, but they discover later through old family photos that the apparition is that of a long-dead relative. Others may report "mist" leaving the body of a dying loved one, as did the writer Louisa May Alcott, who recorded the death of her sister Elizabeth in her private diary. As she wrote of the event,

A curious thing happened, and I will tell it here, for Doctor G. [Dr. Christian Geist of Boston] said it was a fact. A few moments after the last breath came, as Mother and I sat silently watching the shadow fall over the dear little face, I saw a light mist rise from the body, and float up and vanish in the air. Mother's eyes followed mine, and when I said, "What did you see?" she described the same light mist. Doctor G. said it was the life departing visibly.[5]

Other versions of SDEs include precognitive experiences, sometimes referred to as crisis apparitions, in which a healthy person experiences an apparition of a loved one who is dying unexpectedly, often at a great distance. Such an event can happen in the form of a dream or a hyperreal experience in which the deceased person actually seems to be standing in the same room.

Types of Shared Death Experiences

This book deals largely with the different types of SDEs, including descriptions of the experiences along with case studies that provide living proof that consciousness survives bodily death. More specifically, I refer to the seven experiences outlined in this book that build strong evidence for an afterlife, which include all or some of the following elements:

- separation of mind and body
- return from apparent death
- psychic communication
- significant increase in knowledge as result of being near death

Most important, there must be a credible witness to each of these elements, which is how we make certain they are objective and provable. The goal is to present objective evidence that could stand up in court, that is if courts dealt with issues of the afterlife.

Following are the seven types of SDEs that in my estimation yield proof of an afterlife. They are the seven reasons to believe in life after life. There are undoubtedly several more reasons to believe in an afterlife, depending upon your belief system. That said, the ones I have chosen to focus on are the ones I believe to provide the most solid form of proof.

Reason #1: Out-of-Body Experiences

Many of those who have near-death experiences report having an out-of-body experience (OBE), in which they observe their bodies and other events around them as they linger on the border of life and death. Many of these OBEs involve the subject hovering above their body, witnessing events around them, such as medical personnel as they work feverishly to restart a heart, or stem the flow of severe bleeding, or correct some other potentially fatal condition. And when they return to consciousness, they recount in convincing detail what they saw and heard as the doctors and nurses fought to save them.

OBEs are magnificent and amazing, especially if the near-death experiencer (NDEr) is able to recount events they should not have been privy to in an unconscious state. If they can recount these events to the satisfaction of those who can confirm them, then this objective recall is a gold standard of consciousness research.

Here's a thrilling OBE case told by a woman who nearly drowned in a boating accident. This case is from the archives of the Near Death Experience Research Foundation (NDERF), an organization run by Jeffrey Long, MD, and his wife, Jody, that has collected and studied accounts of near-death experiences from all over the world.

The next thing I knew I was a hundred feet above the river, looking down at the raft stuck against the rocks below. I saw the two men in the raft looking for me to come out from underneath. I saw the other woman, who had been in our raft, downstream, clinging to a rock. I watched my husband and my teenage sister, who had rafted, without incident, down the rapids ahead of us, come running back up the hill to find out why all the debris was floating down the river. We had taken everything out of their raft and put it into ours in case they flipped over, but they went down so easily, we just jumped in to follow them down.

From above, I watched my husband climb onto a rock in the river. He couldn't hear what the two men still in the raft were shouting to him over the roar of the water. He had no idea where I was or what had happened, but he knew I was missing. He looked as if he wanted to jump in to try to find me and I suddenly found myself at his side, trying to stop him because he wasn't much of a swimmer and I knew there was no point. When I reached out to stop him, my hand went right through him. I looked at my hand and thought . . . oh, my god, I'm dead![6]

Many researchers feel that out-of-body experiences at the point of death are proof that a soul can leave the body. Some researchers have stuck their necks out to say that accurate OBE experiences are proof of a supreme being. This may or may not be true, but what can be said for certain is that OBEs are events that are beyond the researcher's intellectual and scientific capabilities at this time. Regardless, there are many in the field of afterlife research trying to study them. You will read more about this in chapter 2.

Reason #2: Precognitive Experiences

Precognitive experiences, also known as crisis apparitions, is when a healthy person experiences the apparition of a loved one who is in a severe crisis or is dying. This visionary encounter is usually perceived as being so real that it seems as though the person in crisis is actually standing in the same room. It can also take place as an auditory experience, in which the dying person speaks to the perceiver.

Here is a case involving a woman I'll call Betsy and her husband, Bob, in this retelling. Bob had had early-onset dementia for several years and was not doing well when this SDE took place.

Oddly enough, the SDE did not yet have anything to do with him, but with his mother, who was dying in a local hospital. Betsy was extremely close to her mother-in-law, so her days were split between caring for both her loved ones. Needless to say, she was living under a cloud of extreme mental stress.

When her mother-in-law was actively dying, Betsy hired a nurse to care for her husband, and she spent most of her time with her mother-in-law at the hospital. One night, Betsy found herself in a tunnel that had suddenly manifested in the hospital room. At one end of the tunnel stood a much-younger-looking version of her mother-in-law seemingly beckoning to Betsy and saying in a clear and strong voice, "Come on, it's great in here." Betsy refused the invitation, waving her arms and declaring that she had to stay and care for her ill husband.

Suddenly Betsy realized that her mother-in-law was not beckoning to her but to Bob, who was standing behind Betsy also in the tunnel.

Bob also looked younger and healthier. He was noticeably happy as he looked at this healthy version of his mother.

A short time later, the tunnel closed, and the mother-in-law passed away. Betsy found herself standing alone in the room, wondering what had happened.

Within a month, Bob came down with a respiratory infection, and he died too.

For Betsy, these events were both puzzling and soothing at the same time. As she interpreted the events, her mother-in-law knew that Bob was near the end of his life and was welcoming him into a "new life." Betsy said to me, "It was like she was in a swimming pool shouting to her son, 'Come on in, the water's fine.' I miss them both, terribly, but at the same time, this experience was deep and wonderful."[7]

Precognitive experiences are remarkable and varied. And they are plentiful, which makes them so fascinating that the late Erlendur Haraldsson, a noted apparition researcher from Iceland whom you'll meet in chapter 3, called them "the most convincing of afterlife proof."[8]

Reason #3: The Transforming Light

Does having a death experience change a person in a visible and positive way? To test this question, a team of researchers in Seattle came together to answer a single question: Are there transformative effects from death experiences that can be documented and observed?

After a complex study of more than four hundred people who'd had NDEs, the results showed a variety of objective and profound changes in the personality of the test subjects, including a decrease in death anxiety as well as a higher zest for living, over those who had not experienced an NDE. Also found were factors such as the development of higher intelligence and an increase in psychic abilities.[9]

To keep from sounding blindly optimistic, it is fair to point out that not all change is positive, even when it appears to be from the data gathered by researchers. Some people change so much from their NDE that they are no longer the same person. It's hard to believe, but a spouse who used to be demanding and short-tempered can become, after their NDE, kind and forgiving, which might be more of a change than a marriage can handle. It might be too much for a career, too, if a professional known as being one way suddenly changes in an extreme other direction.

A story heard from fellow researcher Melvin Morse is a prime example of what I'm talking about. A lawyer I'll call David came to Dr. Morse with a perplexing problem. After a challenging day in court, he had a heart attack at his office that nearly killed him. He was rushed to the hospital where the insertion of stents into occluded heart arteries saved his life. When he came out of the hospital several days later, he arrived back at work with a healthier heart and a healthier outlook on life.

This new outlook on life didn't bode well for his career. He was known as "The Hammer" at work because of his ability to pound people during depositions, even if they didn't deserve it. That was before his NDE. Now, post-NDE, he was a teddy bear who was no longer interested in driving people to tears.

With his inborn talents for conflict now gone, David was no longer of use to the firm and was asked to leave.

"I just didn't have it anymore," he said. "I worried for a while before I came to the realization that this was a good thing. The heart attack made me realize that the old me wouldn't last much longer, and I looked at this as a blessing."[10]

David moved to a smaller firm where he worked in family law and was able to spend eight hours per day at the office instead of his previous twelve-hour days.

For many like David, this change can be as extreme as those found in fiction, which is why I sometimes call this transformation the Scrooge Syndrome, because of the before-and-after change that resembles that of Ebenezer Scrooge's in Charles Dickens's classic novel *A Christmas Carol*.

Reason #4: Terminal Lucidity

Terminal lucidity (TL) is defined as a flash of lucidity and vigor that takes place shortly before death. It sometimes happens in the absence of detectable brain activity. In other words, those who are brain-dead can suddenly re-emerge from apparent death, shocking their loved ones and hospital staff with a return befitting Lazarus, albeit brief. Patients who are brain-dead make a profound temporary comeback, speaking clearly about specific things (family matters, for instance) despite EEGs showing that the brain itself is not functioning. It is as though the brain has been bypassed by a consciousness that does not require gray matter.

What does that mean? Does it mean the gray matter of the brain is not required for the production of consciousness? That the brain and mind really do operate separately and that TL is an observable means of witnessing separation of brain and mind? And if that is the case, does such a separation mean that consciousness survives bodily death?

Even the great psychologist Carl Jung noticed the irony in brainless consciousness when he said, "Total loss of consciousness can be accompanied by perceptions of the outside world and vivid dream experiences. Since the cerebral cortex, the seat of consciousness, is not functioning at these times, there is as yet no explanation for such phenomena."[11]

In my opinion, TL cases provide clear evidence that dualism occurs and that there is some kind of separation of the mind from the body that indicates consciousness does not require the physical brain to function. In fact, some cases of TL indicate that the actual brain itself may get in the way of a functioning mind.

Terminal lucidity is clearly a shared death experience simply because it is witnessed by one or more person(s) shortly before bodily death, and oftentimes after cognition and brain function are gone, indicating a return to life that is highly unlikely if not impossible. As one TL researcher said, "NDEs and terminal lucidity are the opposite. The NDE is about leaving, and TL is about coming back."[12] It appears that what is "coming back" to life is the person's soul.

Reason #5: Spontaneous Muses, Healings, and Skills

Many who have near-death experiences report visiting halls of knowledge where they are exposed to—or some say they are even downloaded with—what seems to them to be all the information of the world.

There is a small percentage of these NDErs who return with new talents—increased skills and intellect—as result of this powerfully transforming encounter. Others are healed physically or mentally by this exposure. Many return with guardian angels who stay with them for life as spiritual consultants.

With some, these changes can be quite dramatic. Perhaps they change professions or become obsessively interested in spiritual matters while others become accomplished artists such as painters, writers, actors, and so on. But the experience can also affect other aspects of personality as well. This change is observed by those around the experiencer and is so profoundly obvious that all who know them see a quantifiable difference. By the mere act of witnessing such a change, the observer is witnessing a shared experience.

How could such a thing happen, especially almost instantly? Chapter 6 introduces you to two successful medical doctors and others whose lives changed for the better when they nearly died.

Reason #6: Light, Mist, and Music

Phenomena of light and mist appearing in the vicinity of a dying person have also been reported throughout history. Such reports continue all the way into the modern era. Although I have not experienced any of these personally, I have been present for emotional exchanges between people who have.

One day in the Macon, Georgia, hospital I worked in, I walked in on a conversation between a surgery tech and an intern about this very subject. The intern had heard the buzz going around that a nurse on the night shift had seen a patient lightly glow as she died. Shaken by this unusual event, the nurse reported the event to the head nurse, who shared it with another nurse, and so on. Eventually the story got to the intern, who was fascinated that something so astounding could not be found in his medical books.

The surgical tech responded that he had been on staff for several years and had heard a few such stories. He was no longer impressed but wished he could see the phenomenon himself.

I was interested in what they were saying and began to ask questions of my own. But before the tech could answer them, a nurse who had come into the room interrupted with her own opinion.

"They are just optical illusions," she declared, putting an end to the conversation.

A few years later, I heard a different opinion issued by an oncologist in Charlotte, North Carolina. He was tending to a patient with end-stage cancer when the heart monitor began to beep and the screen registered a flat line, indicating an absence of heartbeat. As the doctor began checking the electrodes to make certain they were still connected, the patient lit up. The doctor was surprised at what he had witnessed, he told me, and had pondered it many times in the months since the event.

"I don't know what it was, but I know for sure it happened," he said. "But in truth, I have no reason to believe it was the soul I saw. All I can say for sure is that it was a light."

Mysterious lights seen in the rooms of the dying may come from multiple sources. Either they originate seemingly independent of the body of the dying or they originate from that body. People may see a halo or other light shining around the head of the dying, or they see mist or shapes leaving the body. In some cases, these shapes may assume a human form.

In addition, NDErs sometimes report hearing inexplicably beautiful music during their experience. But once again, it is something only they hear, and that makes it a strictly subjective experience. This is not the case in the SDE, where the sound of music is sometimes heard by many if not all of those at the deathbed. Cases like these are remarkable in that they demonstrate most compellingly that there is something going on that cannot be attributed solely to the dying brain of the patient.

One of the most famous cases occurred in the seventeenth century at the deathbed of German writer Johann Wolfgang von Goethe, when five people heard inexplicable spherical music in his house yet could not trace its origin.[13] In another astonishing case, a deaf-mute person indicated he heard music, as did the bystanders at his deathbed,[14] a recovery of senses that resembles blindsight, reports in which blind people claim to see during NDEs.

Light, mist, and music are paranormal phenomena frequently seen by those watching over the dying. They are often among the subjects discussed at conferences yet are rarely the subject of attention by researchers in the field of death studies. They are important because they show that some essence of the dying has not only survived but is manifesting itself to others.

Reason #7: The Psychomanteum

Independently and all over the world, in primitive times and modern, intentionally and by accident, people have discovered that by gazing into a clear depth, they can open a door into a visionary world and see departed loved ones again.

As a psychiatrist, I was most intrigued by any possible therapy that this could accomplish. If a reunion with the departed would assuage grief, then reunion with the departed was what I wanted to offer. And if it meant going back into history to find ways to do it, then I was willing.

I studied all the methods I could find, especially those of the ancient Greeks, who created a chamber called the psychomanteum that was very effective in reconnecting with the dead. I even went so far as to build a psychomanteum at my Creekside home in Alabama. When I opened it to clients, I discovered a bizarre truth: a large percentage of those who went through the gazing process were meeting with their departed loved ones. Some of the meetings were so vivid that the participants insisted their loved ones had returned in the flesh.

One such example was a certified public accountant from New York City who came to commune with his departed mother and declared,

> There is no doubt that the person I saw in the mirror was my mother! However, she looked healthier and happier than she had at the end of her life. Her lips didn't move, but she spoke to me, and I clearly heard what she had to say. She said, "I'm fine," and smiled happily. I stayed as relaxed as I could. . . . My hands were tingling, and I could feel my heartbeat pick up speed. . . . I said, "It's good to see you again," and she replied, "It's good to see you too." . . . I felt her reach out and touch me, as though she was reassuring me that she was fine in this new place. That was it. She simply disappeared. Just from what I saw and heard, I can see that she is no longer in pain like she was in her last days here on earth. . . . That alone removes a lot of stress from my life.[15]

Stories of real encounters came out of the psychomanteum weekly. Some clients reported lengthy conversations, while others said their loved ones came out of the mirror (which is what I used as a gazing medium) and sat with them. Sometimes the loved one would not appear in the psychomanteum but would appear later when the client returned to their hotel room. One woman's son appeared at her hotel room and held her hand as they spoke at length; then he hugged her tenderly and, she recounted simply, went away. The comedian Joan Rivers came to the psychomanteum and left it weeping after a frank discussion with her late husband, Edgar, who had committed suicide. She described her experience through sincere and intense tears but wouldn't tell me exactly what Edgar had said, only that she now knew the pain of why Edgar had killed himself.[16] Oprah, on the other hand, was stunned with confused disbelief when a retired air force colonel who volunteered to go through the psychomanteum told the audience of her mother coming out of the mirror and sitting so close to her that she could feel her presence.[17]

I was frequently encouraged by friends to plant a concealed camera in the psychomanteum, but of course my oath to patient confidentiality prevented such a breech. As a result, all claims of encounters with "the real" departed loved one fell into the realm of a subjective encounter for me, one that I could only hear about but not witness for myself.

That all changed when a woman who came to see her late daughter took a photograph of three orbs that appeared to her in broad daylight, orbs that contained the essence of her daughter. It was then that I saw the psychomanteum in a completely different way, revealing to me a level of proof of soul survival.

A View of the Soul in Action

Shared death experiences make it clear that consciousness is not just a chemical reaction in the brain, separate from the spiritual. Shared death experiences are proof that near-death experiences are more than oxygen deprivation to the brain. Bystanders to death can have the same transcendent experiences as those who are dying or who are retrieved from a close call with death. This new development—the aggressive study of shared death experiences—puts us at the frontier of the afterlife.

2

Reason #1: Out-of-Body Experiences

We have to recognize that we are spiritual beings with souls existing in a spiritual world as well as material beings with bodies and brains existing in a material world.

—John C. Eccles

Most of those who have out-of-body experiences (OBEs) are convinced that their consciousness left their body and they witnessed events they should not have seen in their unconscious state. From this movie-camera viewpoint, they could see and hear earthly events. If they were in an operating room, they might have been able to rise above themselves and see the doctor perform a life-saving procedure that they could later describe in detail. This sense of leaving one's body is reported by as many as 50 percent of those who have an NDE and are a leading indicator that there is truly a mind *and* body.

An OBE Review

To better understand the variety of OBEs that we researchers learn about, I have included several examples here. These examples are aimed at showing not only that OBEs occur to a variety of people under a diverse set of conditions but that they reveal themselves in a number of ways and have an immediate psychological effect on those who have them and on those who witness them as shared death experiences (SDEs).

A Royal OBE

A typical example of an OBE took place in 1984 to King Hussein of Jordan, who began hemorrhaging from a blood thinner he took for a heart condition. His doctors were summoned, and before they could reverse the effects of the blood thinner, he had gone into shock and his heart had stopped. Horrified, his doctors worked faster. His wife, Queen Noor, later described in her memoir, "My husband was, for all intent and purposes, dead."[1]

The doctors successfully restored his heartbeat. A few days after his cardiac arrest, Hussein declared the experience to be quite pleasant. As the queen later recounted him saying: "I felt no pain, no fear, no worries. . . . I was a free spirit, floating above my own body. It was rather a pleasant feeling, really."[2]

CT Scan Gone Bad

Another OBE happened to a woman named Andrea during a CT scan. Here, in her own words, is what happened to her. Her observations were later confirmed by every one of the medical personnel attending to her:

> After I was injected with the contrast dye, I started sneezing uncontrollably. The scans were performed, and the nurse informed me that it was time for me to leave. At this point I couldn't speak or breathe. I then passed out, and the nurse frantically called for the code blue team. By the time the code blue team arrived, I guess I was "dead." I saw the team enter and surround a person; at least that's what I thought at the time. It never dawned on me that the other person was me. I was very calm but felt terrible for the lady (me) as the code blue team struggled to get her heart started. I saw "me" being intubated and chest compressions as they tried to revive me. I saw my catheterization and everything else around me. Forty-five min-

utes later my heart started to beat on its own. I was pulled back into my own body.[3]

Some have even "separated" from their body during surgery and witnessed in detail special tools and complex procedures being used on their heart or brain. Since the anesthetic is believed to render a person devoid of consciousness, surgeons often report being stunned by the accuracy with which a patient reports what took place in the conscious world around them while they were believed to be unconscious.

Healthy to Dead and Back Again

Sometimes proof of being out-of-body comes from a third-person perspective, someone who witnesses the person as they are out of their body. As you can imagine, OBEs like these are extremely rare events that are treated with reverence by the death study community.

One such case came to me out of the blue. After a lecture in Italy, I was approached in the back of the hall by a very serious man, a surgeon, it turned out, who had been puzzled for some time by an event that took place during a surgery he was performing.

He was doing an elective procedure on a young man who was in excellent health, he said. The surgery was something he had performed many times before and there was no reason to think that anything bad would happen. But it did. Shortly after the surgery started, the patient had a cardiac arrest that the surgeon couldn't reverse. He started with chest compression, and when that failed, he brought out the electric paddles to shock the heart into action. Nothing happened. The young man's heart remained static. The surgeon said he had that sinking feeling that this patient was not going to make a comeback. *Oh my God, how did this happen?* he asked himself. *And what am I going to say to the family?*

Suddenly, as he was trying to cope with this agonizing situation, the door to the operating room swung open and a woman rushed him. So frantic was she that, at first, he thought a mental patient had escaped from another part of the hospital and was attacking him.

The surgeon recounted her shouting, "Don't let my husband die! My husband is not dead. I was out in the waiting area when my husband suddenly came to me. He said you think he's dead! He told me I should come in here and tell you that he is not dead."

The surgeon said he did not remember resuming the resuscitation, only that he went on "automatic pilot" and continued with great vigor to stimulate the patient's heart. Soon the patient's heart started beating again.

After the patient was taken to a recovery room and regained consciousness, he told the doctor what had happened from his point of view. "I was above my body looking down at you, and I could tell that you thought I was dead. I kept trying to say to you, 'I'm not dead, I'm not dead,' but you wouldn't hear me. So I went into the waiting room and told my wife to come in here and let you know I am not dead."[4]

Common and Powerful

The stories I've just shared are many things: incredible, hopeful, fascinating. But primarily they are objective stories suggestive of the soul's ability to leave the body and communicate a message, in these cases, a powerful one: *I am still alive.* Together, provable OBE stories can be enough to convince many of us, including the most skeptical of scientists, that there is something to the notion that the body may die but the soul lives on.

Since stories are such important tools in explaining separation of consciousness, I include several here that clearly illustrate objective OBEs and why they are so important in defining consciousness. A few are from the archives of the Near Death Experience Research Foundation (NDERF), an organization that has successfully collected accounts of near-death experiences from all over the world. The others are from my own archives.

Witnessed His Cardioversion

Here is a story told to me by Melvin Morse, MD, about a seven-year-old boy who had a cardiac arrest in the lobby of a hospital. This case study is written from my notes taken while interviewing Morse:

The boy remembered being in the hospital lobby and then feeling a sinking feeling "like when you go over a bump in a car and your stomach drops out from under you." He heard a "whooshing" noise in his ears and people talking. He then was floating against the ceiling, looking down at his body below him. The room was dim, and his body was illuminated by a soft light. He heard a nurse say, "I wish we didn't have to do this," and observed ongoing cardiopulmonary resuscitation. He saw a nurse "put some grease on [his] body," and then she "handed paddles to the doctor." The paddles were placed on his body and when "the doctor pressed the button, [he] was suddenly back in [his] body, looking up at the doctor."

He perceived significant pain as the shock went through his body and stated that he had recurrent nightmares of the pain of this technique, known as cardioversion.

Nurses present stated that he opened his eyes after cardioversion and said, "That was really weird. I was floating above my body and was sucked back into myself."[5]

OBE Confirmed

Here is a case told to me by Viola Horton, a woman who had emergency surgery, plus her entire family, and her doctor, an emergency room physician. This was one of the first confirmable OBEs I heard and is the one that convinced me that consciousness could roam and return to the human body.

Viola was able to leave her body, then leave the operating room, and confirm her OBE by describing what she saw and heard in other parts of the hospital. According to her doctor's account of what Viola shared, Viola left her body and went into the waiting room and saw her young daughter wearing mismatched plaids. Later when Viola told her family about her experience and the fact that she had seen the girl in mismatched clothing (she'd dressed hastily to get to her mother's side), they knew that she must have been in that waiting room with them. While in the waiting room, she also saw her brother-in-law on the pay phone. She approached him to try to make contact and could hear his conversation.

"Well, I was going out of town to see Uncle Henry," he was saying to a business associate. "But it looks like my sister-in-law is going to kick the bucket, so I'd better stick around and be a pallbearer."

She told all of this to the doctor a few days later. Her family doubted these events until she turned to her brother-in-law and said, "Next time I die, you go off to see Henry because I'll be just fine."

They had all heard what he said on the telephone and were as stunned as he was embarrased when they realized she had seen and heard everything that had been said and done.[6]

An Out-of-Body Meeting

Here is a unique OBE that involved communications between a brother and sister, each in separate hospitals and each near death at the same time, the brother from heart problems and the sister in a diabetic coma. I heard this OBE from the brother, a soldier at Fort Dix in New Jersey. I want to note that this case study is one that I used in *Glimpses of Eternity* and have decided to use it here as well because of its complex nature:

I left my body and went into the corner of the room, where I watched doctors work on me down below.

Suddenly I found myself in conversation with my sister, who was up there with me. I was very attached to her, and we were having great conversation about what was going on down there when she began to move away from me.

I tried to go with her, but she kept telling me to stay where I was. "It's not your time," she said. "You can't go with me because it's not your time." Then she just began to recede off into the distance through a tunnel while I was left there alone.

When I awoke, I told the doctor that my sister had died. He denied it, but at my insistence, he had a nurse check on it. She had in fact died, just as I knew she did.[7]

I was near Fort Dix when I heard this story and had some free time in which to visit with the attending physician on this case. The doctor not only confirmed the story but added how it had changed his own professional demeanor. He said the case seemed so far out that he would ordinarily have passed on investigating it. After all, he was a busy army doctor with a full load of patients, and this felt more like a dream instead of an actual event. But after the patient's bizarre vision proved to be real, the doctor decided to no longer be skeptical of stories like these. He made a promise to himself to listen to each patient's story and assess it from a different point of view.

As I recall him saying, "Things happen that are not according to the medical books, and I don't want to miss the opportunity they give me to learn."[8]

The Investigators

There have been accounts of OBEs for thousands of years. Images of them appear in hieroglyphs in Egypt, in which the spirit double of a deceased person is seen to be leaving its body. Much later, the ancient Greeks tackled the OBE philosophically, thanks to Hermotimus, an 800 BCE figure who became famous for being able to get out of his body at will and travel to distant locations. This made Hermotimus a sensation among philosophers who believed his ability to leave his body proved the existence of both a mind and a body.

The notion that the mind can be separate from the body opened the door to what is now known as the mind-body problem, the study of the relationship between the mind and the body, or if a non-material mind even exists.

Modern Science and the OBE

In contemporary times, there have been several researchers who have applied the scientific method to the study of OBEs. Early on, I was not one of them. When I wrote *Life After Life*, I made it clear to the readers that this was not a work of science. Rather, it was a work of observation, plain and simple. If a scientific study were to be done, I said, somebody else would have to do it.

Shortly after the book came out, cardiologist Michael Sabom, MD, accepted that challenge. He was in the room when Sarah Kreutziger, a psychiatric social worker at the University of Florida in Gainesville, presented an adult Sunday school class on my book. Her presentation seemed to impress everyone at the class except Sabom, who didn't believe that the accounts of near-death experiences in the book were real.

Later that week, Kreutziger telephoned Sabom and told him that the pastor had heard about her class and wanted her to deliver it to the entire church. She asked Sabom to join her.

He agreed to her offer with one addition: he would ask several of his heart attack patients if a near-death experience (NDE) had happened to them during their resuscitation. Kreutziger agreed and said she would ask some of the patients she dealt with if they had ever experienced any of the elements of the NDE found in my book.

This would become a longer-term "church study" (as I called it). For it, Sabom insisted to Kreutziger that they systematically collect objective observations in a rigorous and unbiased method, aka the scientific method. He felt, and correctly so, that my method of gathering case studies in *Life After Life* had been too casual and unsystematic for his strict medical approach.

The two researchers agreed to use patients who were physically near death, meaning a patient who'd had an extreme physiologic catastrophe who would not be expected to live without medical intervention.

Each patient who'd had a confirmed near-death experience had their experience compared to those outlined in my book. Kreutziger and Sabom recorded the patients' educational, occupational, social, and religious backgrounds and analyzed the content of their NDEs against those background influences.

Most interesting to Sabom were the OBEs that so many of my subjects reported. They claimed to recall many visual details, even though they were unconscious and should not have been able to recall anything at all.

The duo conducted their study in several church and civic group classes, picking up a number of case studies from attendees. Krutziger moved to Louisiana to complete her doctoral studies, and Sabom moved on to Emory University School of Medicine and a position as staff physician at the Atlanta Veterans Administration Hospital, where he had access to many near-death survivors. This new hospital assignment greatly expanded the size of his study population.[9]

Sabom and I, along with Kenneth Ring, PhD, Bruce Greyson, MD, and John Audette, would eventually join forces to create the International Association of Near-Death Studies (IANDS) in 1977, an organization aimed at studying the near-death experience.

Sabom launched the Atlanta Study in 1978, an investigation into near-death experiences that focused primarily on OBEs. In proving that consciousness had truly left the body at the point of clinical death (defined as the point at which a patient's external signs of life are absent and have not yet been successfully reversed), Sabom compared the patient's recollection of what they had seen against the medical staff's notes of what had taken place during the act of resuscitation. Because Sabom is a cardiologist, most of his case studies came from individuals who had experienced cardiac arrests. This was a plus, given that most agree that a patient whose heart stops is near death.[10]

I must admit I felt a great sense of relief in the findings of Sabom and Krutziger. Not only were they excellent researchers dedicated to the scientific method but they were both willing to bury their bias and accept the results of their research. Before the Atlanta Study began, Sabom did not trust the conclusions I wrote in *Life After Life*. He actually thought I had fabricated most of the case studies. Krutziger believed the conclusions I had reached. Yet when it came to collecting and analyzing the case studies, both researchers kept their opinions to themselves, basing their conclusions on the results of their study.

Because of their meticulous work, Sabom and Krutziger gathered some excellent case studies, like the four provable OBE cases listed here. These are cases in which the patients' consciousness separated from their bodies and they were able to "see" and later describe what the medical team caring for them was doing. Each of these cases were told by the patient in their own words and then authenticated by the attending physicians.

Unconscious Sight

Following his cardiac resuscitation, a man described the procedure: "And when I mentioned a couple of things that he [the doctor] had done, really that's what made him think, 'Well, I did do that. I know you were unconscious, so you must have seen.' There were a few things, and I don't remember them now, that he felt like I just had to have seen or would not have known that he had done them."[11]

Doctor Said Impossible

In an out-of-body state, a patient told his doctor what he had seen during a cardiac arrest:

When Dr. B [saw] me, he told me I had a close call and died and all that stuff. I told him, "Dr. B, I couldn't have died. I knew everything

that went on." I told him when he came up under my right arm-
pit and changed his mind and went to the other side. He said it was
impossible and that I couldn't have possibly seen that and that I was
legally dead at that time. He just shook his head. He just couldn't
understand it. And I asked, "Am I right?" He said, "Yes, you're
right!" He just shook his head and went walking off.[12]

Flatlined

A fifty-year-old real estate broker described his cardiac arrest and NDE:

Then I got my chest pain and passed out. I don't remember anything
for a while, and the next thing I remember I was hanging on the ceiling looking down on them working on my body. . . . [The nurse] put
a needle in there and was shooting it into the IV. . . . Everything was
there just like it always was there—the nightstand, the chair, everything I could think of. . . . It looked like he [the doctor] had one hand
on my chest and he kept hitting it real hard. I could see the bed moving up and down. . . . [The cardiac monitor] wasn't running at that
time. The red light was on and there was a line across. . . . It seems
that whatever they had done got the monitor running again. That's
when I got back in bed.[13]

Perfect Reentry

A man recalled his heart attack:

I couldn't stand the pain anymore. . . . And then I collapsed. That's
when everything went dark. . . . After a little while . . . I was sitting
up there somewhere and I could look down, and I had never noticed
that the floor was black and white tile. That's the first thing I remember being conscious of. . . . I recognized myself down there, sort
of curled around in a half-fetal position. Two or three people lifted

me and put me up on a tray, not a tray but a dolly. . . . They strapped my legs and started moving me. When they first threw me up on the table [the doctor] struck me, and I mean he really whacked the hell out of me. He came back with his fist from way behind his head and he hit me right in the center of my chest. And then they were pushing on my chest. . . . They shoved a plastic tube, like you put in an oil can, they shoved that in my mouth. . . . It was at that point I noticed another table-like arrangement with a bunch of stuff on it. I knew [it] later to be the machine that they thump you with. . . . I could see my right ear and this side of my face because I was facing away. . . . I could hear people talking. . . . It [the cardiac monitor] was like an oscilloscope. It made the same streak, over and over. . . . They put a needle in me. . . . They took it two-handed—I thought this very unusual. . . . [Then they took these] round disks with a handle on them. . . . They put one up here—I think it was larger than the other one—and they put one down here [patient pointed to the appropriate positions on the chest]. . . . They thumped me and I didn't respond. . . . It appeared to me in some sort of fashion that I had a choice to reenter my body and take the chance of them bringing me back around or I could just go ahead and die, if I wasn't already dead. . . . I knew I was going to be perfectly safe, whether my body died or not. . . . They thumped me a second time. . . . I reentered my body just like that.[14]

As added proof of the accuracy of OBE perception, Sabom had patients describe the CPR they had all undergone during their cardiac arrests. Their answers were compared against a group of twenty-five "seasoned cardiac patients" who'd had resuscitations but did not have NDEs or OBEs.[15] The study concluded that those who had NDEs and OBEs offered descriptions far more accurate than those who did not have OBEs, convincing evidence that those OBEs really did offer an accurate visual view of reality.[16]

Further Studies

Another OBE study worth looking at, published in 2006, was conducted by Penny Sartori, who interviewed fifteen near-death experiencers (NDErs), eight of whom reported leaving their bodies.[17] She compared their accounts of what they saw against patients who'd had NDEs but without OBEs. She found the ones who claimed to have left their bodies described highly accurate accounts of their resuscitations while those who did not leave their bodies offered inaccurate descriptions of their resuscitations.[18]

In a particularly arduous study published the following year, Jan Holden, EdD, a researcher and educator from the University of North Texas, gathered all the NDEs accompanied by OBEs that had been published to date in scholarly articles and books.[19] She found that eighty-nine of those cases contained observations of everyday earthly events, while fourteen NDErs described "nonmaterial, nonphysical phenomena" that later could be verified.[20] The study's criteria was so stringent that the OBE observation would be ruled "inaccurate" if a single observation was wrong.[21] Despite the strict criteria, 92 percent of the OBE descriptions were ruled accurate, an overall score that offers proof for the reality of OBEs.[22]

Jeffrey Long, MD, founder of the Near Death Experience Research Foundation (NDERF), published a study on the accuracy of OBE observations during near-death experiences.[23] This investigation reviewed 617 NDEs that were shared on the NDERF website survey.[24] Of the 617 NDEs shared by individuals, 287 NDEs included OBE accounts with enough information to objectively determine the reality of their observations.[25] A review of these 287 OBEs found 280 (97.6 percent) had described ongoing earthly events during their NDEs with entirely realistic observations.[26] From this study group of 287 OBEs, 65 NDErs personally investigated their OBE observation accuracy after recovering from their close brush with death.[27] None of these 65 out-of-body experiencers (OBErs) found any inaccuracy in what they observed during their NDEs.[28]

Many of these OBEs contained observations that were far outside the realm of the experiencer's daily life. Long included one such case in an award-winning essay entitled "Evidence for Survival of Consciousness in Near-Death Experiences: Decades of Science and New Insights."[29] In this essay, he quoted a case from a woman who chose to be identified only by her first name, Kate. She was under general anesthesia, in other words, a drug-induced sleep within which all consciousness is put on hold for the duration of the surgical operation:

> I was on the ceiling looking down at the surgery taking place. I was not distressed. The surgeon asked for an instrument. He got the wrong one, so he threw it on the floor. Then I went down a long tunnel that became increasingly bright. I could hear unbelievable music, and ever since, I have loved music. I came out into a bright place with flowers, trees, and a stream that had a bridge over it. The bridge appeared to be made of intertwined tree trunks. At the other side of the bridge was grandma. Next to her was another woman with brilliant blue eyes, a dark mole near her mouth, and an indented chin. I had never seen the other woman before. When I stepped onto the bridge, grandma told me to go back, as it was not my time. She said that I would eventually come there. Then I felt sad as I desperately wanted to be with her. She had always been there for me when I was a child. Then I felt a huge "whoosh." The next thing I knew was that I had returned to consciousness. My mother, whom I was never close to, was crying by my bed. She said, "We nearly lost you. You have been very sick and unconscious for several days." I said, "I want to tell you something." She said, "No, just rest." I insisted and told her about this experience. She did not believe me until I came to the bridge part. My grandma was her mother. I described the lady with my grandma, and my mother said that she was her grandma who died long before I was

born. When the surgeon came to see me, he told me how sick I had been and how I had died on the table. I told him that I was watching and saw him throw the instrument on the floor. Then I told him the story.[30]

"Kate certainly did not expect to see the surgeon throw an instrument on the floor," wrote Long in his paper. "She also would not have expected to see her deceased great-grandmother who died long before she was born."[31]

Also, Kate was having surgery while under general anesthesia, which means she should not have had a conscious experience, period. On top of that, if she had almost died from a cardiac arrest, then she could not have a lucid, organized experience, especially under general anesthesia. "It should be doubly impossible to have any kind of memory whatsoever from that time," said Long. "And yet scores of near-death experiencers have had OBEs under general anesthesia."[32]

Linked to Universal Wisdom

Many in the medical profession believe general anesthesia to be "the sleep of the dead," where the person under its influence cannot be conscious of anything. Yet the research of Long and others who have studied OBEs contradicts that notion with convincing evidence of a kind of "super consciousness" that can override the anesthetic. This is important to the subject of the soul.

The soul, as Long said, is "a nonphysical essence that continues to exist at bodily death."[33] This essence consists of our memories, personality, and personhood. This is a common definition of the soul. But Long's definition goes further. He has postulated that there is a "piece of us" that is connected to spiritual wisdom, a universal library of spiritual information that can only be accessed through certain types of experiences, one of which is the NDE.[34] Other ways may be exceptional dreams, bursts of insight (those aha moments), déjà vu experiences, or sparks of connection to something beyond ourselves. Very few people make a significant connection with universal wisdom, even if they try through such disciplines as meditation or deep prayer. But it is experiences like the NDE that can trigger that kind of connection, and when it happens, it can lead to OBEs and provide access to mystical experiences, feelings, and information we never knew existed.

These mystical experiences usually require some kind of triggering experience, fear, perhaps, an accident, or a heart attack. When that triggering experience takes place, the universe opens. Sometimes this opening will include an out-of-body experience, where the consciousness seems to leave the body and roam freely in real time. Later some can describe in detail people, places, and things they have never before visited.

This is where wisdom, information, and insights outside of their earthly existence come into play. They become aware of a supreme being in a way that they probably wouldn't have without the OBE. To paraphrase Long, they understand such concepts as connection, unity, and oneness that they weren't aware of before their OBE. All of this has led Long to believe that near-death experiences are co-created, one part the earthly NDE and the other part divine wisdom, with a sense of overwhelming love and intelligence, what many people call the presence of God.[35]

Comments like those don't exactly endear Long to some in the medical research community, especially those who don't feel it is scientifically appropriate to pair words like *soul* or *near-death experiences* with *medical research*. Yet for Long, consciousness—the soul—is that invisible something we know almost nothing about.[36] It is invisible, yet it defines our character, personality, personhood, and our universal connection, yet it seems to exist separate from the physical body.

I'm inclined to agree with much of what Long has to say about the soul. To me, personal identity is more easily conceptualized in terms of the narrative structure rather than an abstract entity like the soul. When new events happen to me and I react with certain choices, opinions, and feelings, I naturally fold them into my continuing life story, my narrative—these are part of my personal identity. Doing so makes the concept of a soul much less abstract.

Not one to avoid intellectual conflict, Long fearlessly engages the skeptics with arguments that aim to shoot down beliefs that OBEs are just made up, fantastic dreams, or false memory.

Skeptics Galore

Skeptics argue that when near-death experiencers confirm OBE observations as accurate, they are just lucky guesses, ones pieced together by fantastic dreams or false memory. As Long attests, "This skepticism is refuted by the consistent accuracy of OBE observations found in multiple large studies. These prior studies included hundreds of entirely realistic OBE observations, with many dozens of OBEs later verified as accurate."[37]

What Long said there is true: skeptics criticize OBE research with the same negativity as they criticize all NDE research. They attempt to brush off even the most meticulous OBE research. I see this as a fear factor among skeptics, the fear that their long-held beliefs will be overturned by research that will force them to examine their own views of the world.

Skeptics believe that there are very few OBEs let alone ones that can be proven. "The vast number of case reports with accurate OBE observations, both previously published and posted on the NDERF website, refute the skeptics," declared Long. "This is further illustrated in over a dozen examples of NDEs with verified OBE observations. . . . It is relatively rare for NDERF to receive an NDE account with an OBE observation that was either unrealistic or later verified as not having occurred."[38]

Skeptics believe that OBEs are "false memories" that arise at the beginning and at the end of NDEs.[39] Wrong again, according to Long. The vast amount of research indicates that consciousness during an

NDE takes place in the middle or throughout the entire experience, even when the NDEr is deeply unconscious. This seems contradictory, but this is one of the mysteries of this phenomenon. "During NDEs, maximal consciousness and alertness is typically when the body is unconscious," Long wrote.[40]

I agree with Long. In all the years I have collected and studied NDEs, it is rare to find a case in which the person having the experience does not describe it as being accompanied by crystal-clear sight and the highest level of conscious awareness they have ever experienced. It's hard to believe this is the case, given that NDErs are unconscious and have their eyes closed. Yet this is certainly part of the mystery of the NDE— the ability to have a clear mindsight and a deeper level of consciousness than they've ever had before.

"With hundreds of accurate OBE observations, we now have substantial evidence from NDEs that consciousness occurs apart from the physical body even when the body is unconscious or clinically dead," wrote Long. "OBE observations far from the physical body during near-death experiences are as accurate as the more common OBE observations close to the body. This evidence from NDEs points directly to the conclusion that our consciousness continues after bodily death, and an afterlife is a reality."[41]

What Leaves the Body?

So, what is it that leaves the body during an OBE? Is it a soul? Yes, says Long, it is the soul.[42] To avoid the hot-button aspect of even mentioning "soul" in a scientific world that generally links "soul" with religion, Long has accommodated the two definitions of the soul presented in the *Encarta World English Dictionary*:

• First the non-religious definition: "The complex of human attributes that manifests as consciousness, thought, feeling, and will, regarded as distinct from the physical body."

- And then the definition that includes religion: "In some systems of religious belief, the spiritual part of a human being that is believed to continue to exist after the body dies."

By adopting these definitions of the word "soul," Long and his colleagues have been able to step around arguments of religious bias that may impede otherwise important research. The results are the five "politically correct" elements that define what "it" is that leaves the body during an OBE:

1. **"It" does not need the body to survive.** NDErs report that they leave their body and the pain and suffering that accompanies it, yet remain conscious of themselves and the world around them.

2. **"It" knows that it comes from a specific body.** Almost without exception, people who leave their body recognize the body they have left. They will almost always take time to examine their earthly host. Most NDErs describe "looking down" and seeing their body in distress. Often a doctor or another trained medical personnel has declared them dead or near dead. They often say they felt bad for their body but recognized it as only an earthly vessel for their true selves.

3. **"It" contains the five senses.** NDErs who leave their body are aware that they still have all five senses. Sometimes these senses are enhanced. Many report crystal-clear vision while others have supernatural hearing.

4. **"It" is free to move and does not seem to be tethered to the body.** Although NDErs do return to their body, there is rarely a sense that they are connected to it when they are outside. Many people travel long distances and are accurately able to recount people, places, and events when they return.

5. **"It" is the vehicle into another dimension.** The person who has an out-of-body experience generally finds themselves going into a tunnel through which they enter into another world where they often see dead relatives, encounter beings of light, and have a life review.[43]

Long's research is impeccable, but what is missing here is commentary on the sheer number of people who have OBEs in the world. About 35 percent of those who have NDEs report having an OBE.[44] Some studies report far higher numbers. And a report compiled by IANDS in the countries of Germany, Australia, and the US revealed that as many as 15 percent of their populations have had NDEs.[45] That translates into millions and millions of OBEs, the mere study of which could answer a variety of questions about the nature of consciousness, remote viewing, remote healings, and more.

A major worldwide study would not only open the door to a variety of mystical events but open the door to understanding the unseen powers of the universe, powers that could change the nature of our senses.

The Best OBE I've Ever Heard

Before leaving this subject, I would like to recount the best OBE I've ever heard, best not only because it happened to a person I greatly respect as being truthful but because research proved his experience to be authentic.

In December 1943, George Ritchie, eventual psychiatrist and author of *Ordered to Return*, signed up for the army and was sent to Camp Barkeley in Texas for basic training. While he was there, he came down with a respiratory illness that worsened and developed into pneumonia with a fever of 105 degrees.

He remembers getting out of his hospital bed and looking at his own body, which was still in bed. When that happened, he knew he was in trouble. He had seen his grandfather's body when he died a few years earlier and knew by his own pallor that he, too, had passed over to the other side.

Except there he was, out of his body, observing his surroundings!

Ritchie walked toward the first person he saw, a ward boy carrying a tray full of instruments. Rather than bump into him, as he was about to do, Ritchie walked through the boy as though he was not there.

Nobody can see me, nobody can feel me, and nobody can hear me, he thought. At that point he decided to leave the grounds of Camp Barkeley, Texas, and go back to Richmond, Virginia, to see his mother.

With just the thought of going to Richmond came an unexpected action. He suddenly had the sense of leaving the ground and zooming off for home. Then another thought came to mind: *If nobody can see, feel, or hear me here, why would they be able to communicate with me at home?*

Ritchie decided to land in a small southern town short of Richmond. Looking down the street, he saw a diner. When a man walked out, Ritchie tried to talk to him, but to no avail. He reached out and touched the man on the cheek, but his hand went through the man's head like it wasn't there.

The sense of invisibility frightened Ritchie, especially since invisible in this case meant he didn't seem to be there at all. What would happen if he couldn't see himself back at Camp Barkeley? Was he permanently detached from his body and all its senses?

With just a thought, he was zooming back to Camp Barkeley where he returned to the hospital ward and the last-known location of his body. The ward was packed with men, all of whom looked the same—sunburned, slim, and with tight, short hair, all traits of recruits in training.

He drifted through the ward in search of himself and saw a body covered with a sheet that was tucked in tightly except for a hand that wore Ritchie's class ring. He had found himself.

Looking down at himself, he noticed a small, bright light next to his head that got brighter and brighter until the room filled with very bright light. Far inside himself, he heard a deep voice that said, "Stand up, stand up! You are in the presence of the son of God."

Around him the hospital totally disappeared, and the view that replaced it was a panorama of everything he had ever done in his life.

The voice continued to speak to him, ask what he had done with his life and most particularly what he had done to improve the quality of love in the world.

His body covered by a sheet and his consciousness talking with God, that could easily have been the end for Ritchie, but it wasn't. The doctor completed the certificate of death and ordered the ward boy to prepare Ritchie's body for the morgue. As he did so, the ward boy thought he detected a slight movement and reported it to the doctor. The doctor returned to Ritchie and again declared him dead. The ward boy returned to the doctor again, said he once more saw Ritchie move, and asked the doctor if he could please inject the young soldier's heart with adrenaline. Perhaps tired of being pestered, the doctor did just that, and Ritchie miraculously came back to life. His medical records say that he was pronounced dead twice, about nine minutes apart.

Truth to Experience

Up until now, this story sounds like fantasy—or really good luck. But it is what happened after he got out of the hospital that speaks truth to his experience. Ritchie was on a bus returning to Richmond when it came into the town of Vicksburg, Mississippi.

"There's a diner down the next street," he blurted out to the acquaintance traveling with him.

"How do you know?" the acquaintance asked.

That was when Ritchie told the story of his near-death experience at Camp Barkeley and his out-of-body voyage. The acquaintance decided to test Ritchie.

What's around that corner? he asked. And what's around that? And over there? Ritchie was able to answer each of the questions asked of him by his fellow traveler. It was his correct answers to these questions that make Ritchie's OBE a shared death experience, one in which his consciousness was able to travel freely and tell someone accurately what he had seen.[46]

Ritchie's story was difficult for some people to believe. When he spoke about this experience, as he often did, mainly to a church audience, there would be a percentage of people in the audience who were vocal about their disbelief. Some, usually men, would loudly proclaim that the story was made up and never took place or that he had embellished a bad case of pneumonia into a fantastical journey that mimicked a biblical parable.

I may have partaken of skepticism myself in those days had I not told my father about Ritchie's story shortly after I first heard it.

When he heard the name George Ritchie, my father, a general surgeon, nodded and looked at me with bemusement. "George Ritchie ... I remember him and his story from my days at Camp Barkeley." My father had gone through his corpsman training at the camp at the same time as the Ritchie incident and said that the story was immediately legendary. Add to that the death certificate signed by the attending physician certifying his first death, and the mountain of proof was a high one.

Plus there was evidence of change in Ritchie himself that made his story even more convincing. In the next chapter, "The Transforming Light," you'll read about mental transformations that take place in those who have had near-death experiences, one of which is the ability to have several times the number of verifiable psychic experiences as the general population. That was certainly true of Ritchie. He was frequently the recipient of psychically sent messages. He found this normal and believed the brain to be a receiver for messages from the Source, his initial name for a higher being. He believed this without question and as a result always followed the orders of the voice in his head.

For instance—and this is truly a bizarre one—he was in Washington, DC, with his wife, Margarite, when he looked at an angry man walking past them on the sidewalk. A voice went off in his head, saying that the man was going to kill someone. Ritchie followed the young man and at the next corner asked him kindly if he was on his way to kill someone. Surprised (to say the least), the man admitted he was on his way that very minute to kill a man who had slighted him. As Margarite told me later, he spoke to the young man for several minutes, and when he felt the man had adequately calmed down and was no longer going to commit murder, he and his wife went on their way.

Ritchie was not surprised by this or other psychic receptions. He read a substantial amount of information about psychic powers, and the more he did, the more religious he became. He eventually concluded that he was being guided by the voice of God and didn't think he was unique in receiving this kind of guidance. As he told me in many of our hundreds of conversations, "When I died, I got closer to the source and that gave me a greater connection than most. But we are all connected to God. He gives us this power. We just need to be open to it."[47]

I will accept that explanation. Many scientists believe we live in an intelligent universe that is permeated by consciousness. I have no reason to doubt that assessment. So, if Ritchie believed that and chose to call the Source God, then it is no more different to me than using the word Source to describe a universe with intelligence. Be it considered Source or God, the universal power we are talking about transcends names yet invites speculation about the powers of mind and the ability of it to function separate from the body.

A Different Energy

This brings us to the words of Wilder Penfield, one of the great neurosurgeons and consciousness researchers of the twentieth century. It was his carefully researched maps of the brain that gave science a deeper understanding of how the brain holds memory.[48] He was among the first neurosurgeons to use electrostimulation in his work to treat epileptic seizures[49] while also finding the seat of consciousness within the structure of the brain.[50]

Yes, Penfield was a genius. Yet despite all his surgical and anatomical successes, he admitted to being totally stumped by the mysticism of it all, namely the connections between the brain and the mind. He said in his memoir, *The Mystery of the Mind*:

> It comes as a surprise now to discover during this final examination of the evidence that the dualist hypothesis [separation of mind and brain] seems the more reasonable of the two possible explanations. . . . The exact nature of the mind is a mystery and the source of its energy has yet to be identified. . . .[51]
>
> Whether there is such a thing as communication between man and God and whether energy can come to the mind of a man from an outside source after his death is for each individual to decide for himself. Science has no such answers.[52]

And that was where Penfield chose to leave the argument.

Why OBEs Indicate an Afterlife

The riddle of out-of-body experiences puzzled Greek thinkers as early as around 600 BCE. Though there are more researchers seriously studying OBEs today than ever before, in my humble opinion, there has been little real progress in understanding out-of-body experiences since Aristotle wrote about them in 300 BCE.

To explain this, I leave open the possibility that the principles of reason as we know them are not currently sufficient to comprehend the relationship between the mind or soul and the body, that there may well be more to the mystery of our nature as self-conscious entities than the rational mind can understand.

In the meantime, an out-of-body experience is often a first step toward a conscious realm of love and light. The fact that so many have found themselves out of their bodies and yet psychically more alive than ever before is encouraging news. But more than this, OBEs add another reason and another layer of confidence in our quest to find support for the prospect of personal continuation beyond death.

3

✳

Reason #2: Precognitive Events

I believe no soul is left to wing its viewless flight to Paradise in solitude.

—Basil Wilberforce

Sir William Barrett, the noted physicist introduced earlier in this book, was known as one of the prime movers in afterlife research. He was a physicist in Dublin, Ireland, and founding member of the Society for Psychical Research (SPR), and there was hardly any aspect of paranormal phenomenon that wasn't thoroughly examined by him.

Yet despite this thoroughness in bringing science to this field, Barrett was frustrated by the public's reception to much of his work. He expressed this frustration in a 1924 speech to the SPR only a year before his death: "I am personally convinced that the evidence we have published decidedly demonstrates (1) the existence of a spiritual world, (2) survival after death, and (3) of occasional communications from those who have passed over," he said. "It is however hardly possible to convey to others who have not had a similar experience an adequate idea of the strength and cumulative force of the evidence that has compelled [my] belief."[1]

I agree with Barrett. It can be deeply frustrating to try to convince some people that there is evidence of the afterlife without those people having witnessed that experience themselves. I know this personally. Early in my research into near-death experiences (NDEs) I was one of the doubters Barrett alluded to. But then when I had one of these paranormal experiences—a precognitive experience, to be exact—I stepped into the ranks of the true believers and have never looked back.

Precognitive Experience Defined

Before going further, it would be best to remind you of my definition of the precognitive death experience, which is when a person unexpectedly sees the death of another person, usually a friend or relative. The seeing of this event takes place as a "knowing," dreams, or visions that provide foreknowledge of a paranormal kind. A more general definition, and one I prefer because of its generality, is that a precognitive experience is simply foreknowledge of a paranormal kind. A definition like this can encompass experiences that may deviate from a stricter definition in which the deceased person seems to appear in the same room.

Parallel Dreams

My own precognitive experience took place early in my first marriage and was one of the saddest yet most mysterious days of my life.

The experience came in the form of two dreams—mine and that of my wife. She was seven months pregnant, and both of us were excited for the child to come. That was why these dreams were so disturbing for us.

In my dream, I was standing behind an OB-GYN, his surgical gown a vivid white and his hair a light blond speckled with the gray of middle age. I did not see his face, but I knew he was fearful of what he saw: a dead child coming out with the umbilical cord wrapped around his neck. He had been strangled. It was my wife delivering the child. I could see her tortured face as the delivery took place.

I awoke.

I sat up and turned to my wife. She was already sitting up and looking at me. Her face was streaked with tears as she told me of the dream she'd just had. It was the same as mine, only she was looking at events from her perspective, 180 degrees opposite of mine. She could see the doctor, masked and looking sad, and me standing at his shoulder, also masked and looking sad. She could not feel pain of the child being delivered, but she could see he was dead.

We didn't sleep that night. Just one of us having such a dream seemed unthinkable. But both having the same dream from a 180-degree change in perspective seemed unimaginable and certainly portended the worst.

Twenty-four hours later, the worst happened. We lost our first baby and witnessed it in much the same fashion as our dual nightmare.

Over the years, I have heard a number of precognitive experiences of all kinds. But never have I heard one involving parallel dreams. For me, these parallel dreams changed my professional life. They broke through the wall of detachment that many doctors have when listening to their patients. My level of empathy went up and with it my focus and concentration on the demands people have when they tell me of their deeply personal paranormal events. Like a heart surgeon who has bypass surgery or an orthopedic surgeon who breaks a femur, I now looked at my area of research through a different set of eyes, eyes that have not only seen but also experienced.

A Familial Knowing

Some precognitive experiences are "knowings" rather than dreams like mine and my wife's. This one was submitted to me from a young woman in Oregon. When she was just seven, she was going to spend the day with her grandfather, Poppy, while her mom took her grandmother, Nana, shopping. Just before stepping out of the car, she asked her mom, "What do I do when Poppy falls?" She told me, "I seemed to know that this day was different from the others—that something would happen." Nothing happened that day, but later that night, Nana called and the girl's mother left and didn't return till the next day. Poppy had had a heart attack and died. The woman said to me:

> I've talked to my mom about that day, and she said that as soon as I asked her about Poppy falling, she knew what I meant, and she knew that I was right—that her dad was going to pass that day. My mom knew before she took the phone from me that it was my Nana calling

to tell us about Poppy being taken to the hospital. She knew that he was gone, even when she and my Nana and uncles were at the hospital waiting for the final word from the doctors.[2]

Types of Precognitive Experiences

Although precognitive experiences are a general term for when a person perceives something that has yet to happen or about which they have yet to be notified, there are several different types of precognitive experiences. For the sake of better understanding, I have done the same things with this fascinating experience as I have with shared death experiences (SDEs), breaking it down into six specific categories. These are not written in stone—other researchers will contribute their own categories, and I welcome that. But these six types are a start for now.

Type #1: Vision Is Not Limited to Only One Person

This type of perception can be through a dream, a waking vision, or an auditory experience. This type of precognitive experience is particularly powerful because, since it is witnessed or received by more than one person, it doubly proves that a vision truly took place.

An example of this type of precognitive experience comes to us from Mr. de Guerin and his sister Mrs. Elmslie, both of whom were questioned by members of the Society for Psychical Research in England, because of what they each, separately, saw at the time of their sister Fanny's death, halfway around the world from them.

Elmslie and de Guerin were both living in China at the time, May 1854, though a good thousand miles apart, Elmslie in Carton and de Guerin in Shanghai.

De Guerin wrote that he was lying awake unable to sleep one hot night when the following happened:

I gradually became aware there was something in the room; it appeared like a thin white fog, as misty vapour, hanging about the foot of the bed. Fancying it was merely the effect of a moonbeam, I took but little notice, but after a few moments I plainly distinguished a figure which I recognized as that of my sister Fanny. At first the expression of her face was sad, but it changed to a sweet smile, and she bent her head towards me as if she recognised me. I was too much fascinated with the appearance to speak, although it did not cause me the slightest fear. The vision seemed to disappear gradually in the same manner as it came. We afterwards learned that on the same day my sister died—almost suddenly. I immediately wrote a full description of what I had seen to my sister, Mrs. Elmslie.[3]

Before his letter could have reached her, he received a letter from her, "giving me an almost similar description of what she had seen the same night, adding, 'I am sure dear Fanny is gone.'"[4]

In a later letter, Elmslie said to her brother: "I do not think I was awake when Fanny appeared to me, but I immediately awoke and saw her as you describe. I stretched out my arms to her and cried 'Fanny! Fanny!' She smiled upon me, as if sorry to leave, then suddenly disappeared."[5]

To the siblings' knowledge, Fanny had not been ill, so they would not have imagined her dying. They later learned that on her deathbed, she talked about her siblings to those around her. "She died," de Guerin wrote, "in Jersey, on the 30th May, 1854, between 10 and 11 at night."[6]

Type #2: The Dying Don't Perceive It

These perceptions may be witnessed only by the living tending to or caring for the dying. One of my favorite stories is this one, about two sisters who had fallen asleep in the bed of their third sister, whom they were tending to because she was dying of pneumonia. Suddenly, as reported by the sisters, a bright light appeared over the bed in which the faces of two deceased brothers appeared. Both of the healthy sisters watched the apparition until it gradually faded and disappeared. The sick sister was asleep during this time and died a few hours later.[7]

Here is another such case study, this one in the words of the hospice worker present for a man's death:

> An old man was dying in our unit, and it was a long, drawn-out affair that lasted into the hours of the morning. At one point a woman was waiting at his bedside. I knew right away she was a spirit, not a bodily person. She said nothing; just looked at the man. She was there for some time, maybe several minutes. In the beginning I was shocked. Then gradually I lost my fear of this spirit. The whole thing was so natural. Finally I turned around right out of the room, feeling like I had intruded on a private moment. I wanted to discuss the incident with a more experienced social worker on the ward, but before I could, she said, "I saw her too. Things like this happen fairly often." I was surprised.[8]

Type #3: Apparitions of Deceased Relatives

Here is a wonderful example of this type, which an SDEr told me about. A bedridden woman passed away after a serious illness. Suddenly, the patient's nurse saw a male figure standing at the woman's bed, looking at her body. The figure looked to be made of flesh and blood, and the nurse initially considered the intruder to be a real person. A short time later, the phenomenon disappeared. Based upon the nurse's description, the family members concluded that it could only have been the woman's first husband, who was already deceased.[9]

Type #4: Apparitions Near and Far

My coauthor, Paul Perry, experienced this when his mother died. I leave the story in his words:

A few minutes before my mother died in Scottsdale, Arizona, as it would turn out, Vernon Neppe, MD, then head of neuro pharmacology at the University of Washington Medical School in Seattle, was reading the Sunday newspaper at his kitchen table when he heard a voice telling him to "call Paul Perry." He ignored the voice until the same voice repeated the command. At that point he called me at my home in Arizona, even though we hadn't spoken in several years.

Neppe asked why he might have received such a command to call me. I had no idea. In fact, I was quite stunned. We hadn't spoken in at least five years, and for that matter, I hadn't even thought about Neppe in as much time. Still, I appreciated the call. Despite its mystery, it gave me a strange sense of comfort to know that somehow, some way, a truly talented expert on the brain and gerontology had been given a supernatural message to contact me.

I told him my mother was dying from dementia and immediately asked Neppe if there were any new medical treatments available. Neppe recommended a variety of treatments, including electroshock therapy, which he had used on an elderly demented woman with a high level of success. As we conversed, I received a phone call and switched over to get it. The call was the nurse at my mother's care center telling me that she had just died.

I was saddened that the call hadn't come earlier when maybe something could have been done to help my mother. But I was heartened that something like the command given to Neppe even happened at all, and that maybe it was just the universe making a 9-1-1 call on her behalf.

Here is a similar case, this from the English researchers Gurney, Myers, and Podmore involving a seven-year-old boy, his aunt, and his father's death, which took place in Hong Kong:

On the night of the 21st August, 1869, between the hours of 8 and 9 o'clock, I was sitting in my bedroom in my mother's house at

Devonport, my nephew, a boy aged seven years, being in bed in the next room, when I was startled by his suddenly running into my room, and exclaiming in a frightened tone, "Oh, auntie, I have just seen my father walking around my bed." I replied, "Nonsense, you must have been dreaming." He said, "No, I have not," and refused to return to the room. Finding that I was unable to persuade him to go back, I put him in my own bed. Between 10 and 11 I myself retired to rest. I think about an hour afterwards, on looking towards the fireplace, I distinctly saw, to my astonishment, the form of my brother seated in a chair, and what particularly struck me was the deathly pallor of his face. (My nephew was at this time fast asleep.) I was so frightened, knowing that at this time my brother was in Hong Kong, China, that I put my head under the bed clothes. Soon after this I plainly heard his voice calling me by name; my name was repeated three times. The next time I looked, he was gone. The following morning I told my mother and sister what had occurred, and said I should make a note of it, which I did. The next mail from China brought us the sad intelligence of my brother' death, which took place on the 21st August, 1869, in the Harbour of Hong Kong, suddenly [of heat-apoplexy].[10]

Type #5: Precognitive Visions Not Always Visual

The best I can tell, these arrive like a burst of intuition, or a "knowing," such that the person receiving it has no doubt that it is true.

Here is such a story from a woman in the Philippines that involves a psychic exchange of information:

My husband, José, was deployed on a mission for the Philippine Air Force, and I was at home with our three young boys. It was late; the boys were asleep, but I was awake watching television. I was falling asleep when a man on the television said something had happened to my husband. I startled awake, and the program that was on didn't have the man and wasn't the news. I knew then that something had happened to my husband, and it was later confirmed that, hundreds of miles away, his plane had been shot down and he had been killed by insurgents.

I later found out that after he died but before anyone had told his mother (who was living with her youngest daughter in America), she started talking about him without any prompting. His sister was trying to figure out how to tell their mother that he was dead, and their mother just started commenting out of the blue about how José likes to do this or José enjoys doing that, as if she knew she needed to remember the small details of her son's life.[11]

Type #6: Not All about Death

Not all precognitive experiences include death foretold. Rather, some, like the story of Olga Gearhardt and her son-in-law, are about life foretold. Olga's story was told to both Melvin Morse, MD, and Paul Perry when they were writing their book *Parting Visions: Uses and Meanings of Pre-Death, Psychic, and Spiritual Experiences* and is considered by the two authors to be among the most amazing precognitive experiences either has encountered, as well as one of the most positive. Here it is:

In 1988 a virus attacked Olga's heart and destroyed much of the muscle. Her heart became so weak that it could no longer beat effectively. The only chance she had for survival was a heart transplant.

Olga was put on the transplant-recipient list at the University of California Medical Center. People who are on this list must be in constant contact with the hospital where the transplant will be done. If a heart becomes available that matches their blood type, it must be implanted within hours of the donor's death for the transplant to be effective.

Olga's entire family was notified of this fact, and they all promised to lend moral support by being there at the hospital during her surgery. Early in 1989, Olga received the call from the hospital that a matching heart had been found. As she and her husband left for the hospital, her children started a telephone chain that notified family members in three states that the transplant was about to begin. In a matter of hours, the waiting room of the hospital was overloaded with Olga's family.

The only member of the family not at the hospital was Olga's son-in-law. Although he loved his mother-in-law, he had a phobia about hospitals and preferred to await the news at home.

Late that evening, her chest was opened, and the transplant was performed successfully. At 2:15 AM she developed unexpected complications, and the new heart would not beat properly. As the medical personnel became alarmed, it stopped beating altogether. It took several hours of resuscitation before her heart finally began functioning properly. Meanwhile the family in the waiting room was told nothing about these complications, and most of them were asleep. About six in the morning, the family was told that the operation was a success but that she had almost died when the new heart failed.

Olga's daughter immediately called her husband at home to tell him the good news. "I know she's okay," he said. "She already told me herself."

He had awakened at 2:15 to see his mother-in-law standing at the foot of the bed. It was as though she was standing right there, he said. Thinking she had not had surgery and had somehow come to his house instead, he sat up and asked her how she was.

"I am fine; I'm going to be all right," she said. "There is nothing for any of you to worry about." Then she disappeared.

The vision didn't frighten the son-in-law, but he did get out of bed and write down the time she appeared to him and exactly what was said.

When the family went to see her, Olga began talking about "the strange dream" that took place during surgery. She said she had left her body and watched the doctors work on her for a few minutes.

Then she went into the waiting room, where she saw her family. Frustrated by her inability to communicate with them, she decided to travel to her daughter's home, about thirty miles away, and connected with her son-in-law.

She told them that she was sure she had stood at the foot of her son-in-law's bed and told him that everything was going to be all right.[12]

This is an amazing story and well-researched, so I have no doubt that Olga and her family were not making it up or fudging the facts. To do so would require someone in the family to have a story that varied from the one told here. But no such discrepancies appeared in any of the stories nor was there any motive to invent such a story. As far as I'm concerned, the only conclusion is the obvious one—that Olga was on a heart-lung machine because her new heart was not functioning properly, and she somehow left her body and was able to communicate with her son-in-law, who was in bed more than thirty miles away.

A Study of Dreamers

The case of Olga and others that Morse was studying led him to ask the question: When is a dream just a dream, and when is it precognitive?[13] To answer that question, two hundred individuals were asked to record every dream they could remember over the next two years. Morse and his team then asked them three simple questions:

- Have you ever had a vivid premonition that something terrible has happened or will happen to someone close to you, and then nothing of the sort happened?
- Have you ever had a feeling or dream or vision that your child or spouse was going to die soon, and then it did not happen?
- Have you ever had the intuition or impression that something was going to happen, and then the event did not happen?[14]

Through an analysis of the dreams that did and did not come true, Morse and his team were able to reliably identify the features of those dreams that would likely be followed by real events and those that were just bad dreams. They then deconstructed dreamlike "visions," looking for common elements that make up a core experience for precognitive experiences. The result was the conclusion that visionary dreams have at least two of the following qualities:

- **A "real" or "hyperreal" quality:** Psychical dreams frequently convey the sense of absolute reality.
- **Sights and sounds superimposed over ordinary reality:** An example of this comes from a woman who had a vivid dream of her father dying suddenly, which he did in reality six days later. When she got up from this dream, she found herself walking through a mist that was rising from the floor and disappeared when she turned on the bedroom light.
- **A unique feeling to the dream that is unlike anything experienced before:** Most dreams are quickly forgotten, but a visionary dream is so vivid it can't be forgotten.
- **A mystical white light or a spiritual being of light:** An experience of light is the hallmark of a very deep experience and is one that greatly transforms the person who has it. Because of these personal transformations, many people call this light "God."[15]

This precognitive research revealed that many visionary experiences are witnessed by two or more people. I call this mind-reach, which means the mind has the ability to both send and receive information. This exchange of mental energy can be assumed (and is by many) when obvious psychic events take place, like knowing a loved one is in distress when they are clearly out of normal range of one's senses. Those are examples of mind-reach, when a logical explanation could be that the minds are connecting with one another.

Could minds connecting over a distance explain precognitive experiences? I don't know. And neither do any of the researchers and philosophers over the thousands of years that they have pondered this question. Somehow mind-reach takes place. We have all experienced it on one level or another. Some call it intuition, defined in the psychological studies as "The ability to understand something immediately, without the need for conscious reasoning."[16] But do we know how intuition and psychic events take place? Alas, the answer is still no. All we have to show for thousands of years of research is speculation. Which is what I am doing right now—pondering the imponderable.

Materialists vs. Dualists

At this point it's useful to talk more about the two major schools of thought on this matter—neither of which have proven answers and both of which continue to engage in a battle of speculation.

I mentioned them in passing earlier, so to refresh our memories: subscribers to the materialism school believe everything is physical. In other words, nothing exists except matter and its movements. They tend to reject things and events they can't re-create or measure, particularly matters of the spirit or soul. In other words, they can accept that there is a place in the gray matter of the brain where a sense of God is activated because neurosurgeons have done that very thing with electricity stimulation, they just wouldn't want to link it with an actual God.

Dualists believe that the body and the mind are separate, meaning that the mind can often exist independent of the brain, possibly even communicating from a distance.

As I've already noted, I would cast my vote with the dualists. I accept that much of the world we live in is unexplained. I dare say that most scientists believe the same, especially since the science of quantum mechanics has unveiled several new rules of physics that seem both spiritual and scientific. And, although we may not be able to see or weigh them, we know that they exist beyond the perception of known measurement.

I think that under extreme situations (death being a most obvious example of an extreme situation), the mind can separate from the body where it is free to go to other places during near-death experiences. So why wouldn't the same apply to human physiology?

Although materialists say that psychic powers cannot be consistently reproduced in a laboratory, does that mean it's a waste of time to explore psychic communications or other events like intuition that are known to statistically exist? Not at all. Perhaps what it means is that we need to find different methods of exploration.

When Carl Gustav Jung spoke before the Society for Psychical Research in 1919, he defended psychic research by saying that psychic events are common; we just don't know why or how they take place. Still, he said, "I shall not commit the fashionable stupidity of regarding everything I cannot explain as a fraud."[17] He left it at that.

And that's where I'll leave it too.

Icelandic Studies

This discussion easily leads to that of apparitional studies, particularly those related to precognitive experiences.

The first extensive study into apparitions was released in 1880 by the Society for Psychic Research, namely Gurney, Myers, and Podmore. Their book *Phantasms of the Living* represented the results of the first major study of apparitions. It wasn't until nearly one hundred years later that Erlendur Haraldsson sought to repeat the work of Gurney, Myers, and Podmore by executing his own National Survey of Apparitions, this in his tiny home country of Iceland.

Erlendur (who dropped his last name) gave a detailed questionnaire to 902 adults, asking for their attitudes toward the paranormal, religion, and other cultural aspects. Out of the 902 adults, only 127 people responded and were able to be interviewed.[18] One of the questions in the survey delved into the recipient's own experiences, asking, "Have you felt as though you were really in touch with someone who had died?" A remarkable 41 percent answered yes when asked if they'd had an encounter with the dead.[19] They also answered questions about the deceased person or persons: Did they know them? Were they relatives, friends, or strangers? How old were they and how had they died? Could they identify the characteristics of the dead person?[20]

Thrilled at the response, Erlendur assembled a team of researchers who then conducted in-depth interviews with all the people in the Reykjavik area who agreed to participate. Cases that were dreams or brought about by mediums were discarded from the study group, since Erlendur wanted all the experiences to be direct personal experiences, and he wanted his interviewees to have been in the waking state when the encounters occurred.

Of the 127 interviewed, 100 fit the criteria for verifiable apparitional experiences. Erlendur was thrilled with the number of verifiable experiences and their quality, but he needed more experiencers to make a significant statistical analysis, at least three times as many.[21]

What came out of this work was the most extensive scientific study ever conducted dealing with contact with the dead. Among other factors, his study revealed types of apparitions, including that 59 percent of apparitional sightings were visual, while 24 percent were auditory, 7 percent were tactile, 5 percent were olfactory, and 16 percent sensed a presence in the room.[22]

Almost half of apparitional experiences took place in full daylight, proving wrong the long-standing belief that darkness is the only time when they occur. Also, about a third of the apparitional experiences took place when the percipient was working or actively engaged, not falling asleep or drowsy as most people would likely have thought. In fact, in nearly 75 percent of the visual cases, the apparition was seen with open, awake eyes.[23]

Erlendur's research revealed a number of other interesting facts. Most of those who claimed to have seen an apparition have seen only one. And those who are bereaved or have a terminal illness are more likely to see apparitions of the dead.[24] Among widows and widowers, about 50 percent are likely to report a hallucinatory experience of their deceased spouse.[25] In only 11 cases out of 73 was the percipient in a state of grief, having recognized the apparition as a deceased loved one, but in 13 of the 73 cases, the percipient did not know that the person who they saw was in fact deceased at the time.[26]

None of the people in Erlendur's study had discussed these apparitional experiences with their physician or clergyman, citing fear of ridicule. Keeping in mind that Erlendur's research is now quite old, I would think people have loosened up about reporting these experiences to most anyone, including doctors and the clergy who now admit to having had several themselves.

As you may have expected, Erlendur's study contained several precognitive experiences. I will recount a few of them here to illustrate the variety of the experiences.

Death at the Sanatorium

A woman was working at the sanatorium in Hveragerdi, Iceland. She invited a patient, Jakob, to visit her husband and her because Jakob was from the same village as her husband. She remembered: "Jakob says 'yes' and seems happy about it. And I say to him: 'You promise to come tomorrow.' 'Yes, yes, I promise,' he says." But then:

> During the night I wake up, and all strength is taken away from me, I just lie there unable to move. Suddenly I see the bedroom door open and on the threshold stands Jakob, with his face all covered with blood. I look at this for a good while unable to speak or move. Then he disappears (and closes the door behind him).
>
> I became my normal self and call my husband. "I can swear that something has happened at the sanatorium," I say. I telephone down there the first thing in the morning and ask about Jakob and if everything is all right.
>
> "No," says the nurse. "Jakob committed suicide in the night."[27]

Luckier than He

A long-standing member of the Icelandic parliament remembered a dear friend, K. K., he'd made while in office:

> One fine day in winter, I went out, as I was used to doing after lunch, to dig (snow) from the stable. When I had dug several shovels out, I suddenly feel that K. K. is standing in from of me, saying a bit strangely to me, "You were lucky, you had good luck." Then he disappeared.
>
> During the evening his death was announced over the radio. I speculated on the meaning of his words. I found out that he had died from a heart attack. He had been transferred to the Reykjavik city hospital, where he died.
>
> I had been there myself one year earlier, or there about, with a similar attack. It was possible to alleviate it, and I could go home. When I connected his words I understood [the meaning of what he said to me.][28]

The Guest Who Never Arrived

The percipient visits his sister at a remote farm where both of them had been brought up and where the sister is still living. They are sitting quietly in the kitchen after lunch when the percipient suddenly sees a man pass by the window. The percipient sees his face and clothing well but does not immediately recognize him. He tells his sister that a guest is coming. When no one knocks on the door, they go out and look around but find no one. There are no trees near the farm; there is good visibility; and it is unlikely that anyone could disappear suddenly. As the percipient describes the man further to his sister both of them recognize him as an old friend living in a village several miles away. Later the same day they learn that this man had died about lunchtime in his village.[29]

Vanishing Grandmother

My wife and I had a girl living with us for about two years. One night, I suddenly woke up from a deep sleep and saw a woman standing beside the bed in a dark costume. She said to me, "My name is Margaret." Then she vanished out the door. I looked at the clock and saw that it was exactly 3:30.

The next day I learned that the grandmother of the girl had died at that time from a heart attack. Her name was Margaret.[30]

The Great Unanswerable

In his reporting of these cases, Erlendur is careful to point out that in about one-third them, another person bore witness to the interviewee's experience, which was approximately the same number as similar studies currently going on in other countries.[31]

"To sum it up," wrote Erlendur of his grand study, "it seems that people can have apparitional experiences under a great variety of circumstances. Judging from the reports we have, it even appears that the circumstances and the state of mind of the percipient may play a minor role in the occurrence of apparitions."[32]

I respect Erlendur and all that he did regarding apparitional research in his eighty-nine years on the earth. However, I think this summation of his study is lacking. It leaves the main question of all paranormal research hanging, namely: How and why do apparitions take place to begin with?

I realize I shouldn't focus on Erlendur's research to give us the answer to these questions because nobody—even history's most notable brains—has been able to shine a light on their mystery. Stephen Hawking, the noted astrophysicist, tells a story related to trying to explain the unexplainable in his book *A Brief History of Time*:

A well-known scientist (some say it was Bertrand Russell) gave a public lecture on astronomy. He described how the earth orbits around the sun and how the sun, in turn, orbits around the center of a vast collection of stars called our galaxy. At the end of the lecture, a little old lady at the back of the room got up and said: "What you have told us is rubbish. The world is really a flat plate supported on the back of a giant turtle." The scientist gave a superior smile before replying, "What is the turtle standing on?" "You're very clever, young man, very clever," said the old lady. "But it's turtles all the way down!"[33]

This story shows the danger of trying to answer the unexplainable, the unanswerable, in front of an audience. It does not explain how the universe exists nor how precognitive experiences occur for that matter.

That said, I will willingly admit that I have no idea how precognitive experiences take place, only that they do, and with enough frequency that they can be considered significant contributors to the proof of life after life because of confirmable communication after death. Beyond that it's turtles all the way down.

4

Reason #3: The Transforming Light

Mankind was my business. The common welfare was my business;
charity, mercy, forbearance, and benevolence, were all my business.
—Charles Dickens

Perhaps the most famous near-death experience in all the world is that of Ebenezer Scrooge, the miserly, angry, dour, selfish, hateful businessman in the novel *A Christmas Carol* by Charles Dickens. In this nineteenth-century novel, Scrooge curses his employees for not wanting to work on Christmas Day and goes home to his dark and gloomy house. Later that night, Scrooge is visited by the ghost of his equally miserly business partner whose angry and dispassionate countenance is doomed to wander the earth for eternity, dragging heavy chains and cumbersome boxes of money he earned in his lifetime. The ghost tells Scrooge that he, too, is doomed to the same unpleasantness in his afterlife unless he changes his hateful attitude toward mankind.

Doubting his ghostly business partner's words, Scrooge insults his old friend, declaring that he may just be "an undigested bit of beef, a blot of mustard, a crumb of cheese, a fragment of an underdone potatoe. There's more of gravy than of grave about you, whatever you are!"[1]

To silence his business partner and confirm his ghostly existence, the apparition rattles his chains and introduces three ghosts: the ghosts of Christmas Past, Christmas Present, and Christmas Yet to Come.

The three ghosts deliver a powerful life review to Scrooge, one that reveals him as being a "tight-fisted ... squeezing, wrenching, grasping, scraping, clutching, covetous, old sinner! Hard and sharp as flint, from which no steel had ever struck out generous fire; secret, and self-contained, and solitary as an oyster."[2]

The sad review of his own life has such a powerful effect on Scrooge that he awakens on Christmas a new man. He becomes a kinder, gentler person who raises the pay of his employees, donates large amounts of money to charity, and most touching of all, becomes like a loving uncle to Tiny Tim, the physically challenged son of his most overworked employee, Bob Cratchit.

What happened to Scrooge certainly had all the elements of a near-death experience, especially the most common element of all—transformation.

Transformation is present in nearly all the near-death experiences (NDEs) I have encountered—specifically and importantly, positive transformation. Whether the NDEr is a Scrooge who likes nothing but their own opinion and their wealth or someone else stuck in an unhelpful cycle, the NDE is transformative. This change is so profound that it is widely visible and therefore a shared death experience (SDE).

I don't mean to imply that an NDE turns a person into a syrupy, uncritical optimist. Although it certainly makes them more positive and pleasant to be around (especially if they weren't that pleasant before the near-death experience), it also leads to an active engagement with the real world. It helps them grapple with the unpleasant aspects of their lives with level emotions and in a clear-thinking way—a way that is new to them.

All the scholars and clinicians I have talked to who have interviewed NDErs have come to the same conclusion: NDErs are better people because of their experience.

The Crisis Experience

Although NDEs are known in psychology as crisis events, they don't have negative effects like some other crisis events might. For instance, a bad combat experience might leave a person stuck at that point in time, or "trapped in the foxhole," as some army psychologists might say. Many combat veterans with post-traumatic stress disorder (PTSD), for example, relive the horrifying scenes of death and destruction that they witnessed years ago in combat. They hallucinate to the point that they can smell the gunpowder and feel the heat of combat. This is a negative response to a crisis event.

Other traumatizing events like floods, tornados, fires, and automobile accidents can leave people overwhelmed and unable to put the event behind them. When that happens, they, too, are emotionally stuck.

A near-death experience is classified as a crisis event—such as a car wreck or a natural disaster—and often caused by one of these. But rather than becoming emotionally stuck, NDErs only respond to take some positive action in their life.

One of my favorite pieces of research on the transformative powers of the NDE came from Charles P. Flynn, a sociologist at Miami University in Ohio, who examined data in twenty-one questionnaires that were administered by Kenneth Ring, a noted NDE researcher, to understand what specific transformations occurred in a set of NDErs. "The available evidence shows," he wrote, "in decreasing order of saliency: greatly increased concern for others; lessened fear of death and increased belief in an afterlife; increased religious interest and feeling, both non-institutionalized and institutionalized; and lessened desires for material success and approval of others."[3]

More complete and current research can be found in the Transformation Study done by researchers in Seattle led by Melvin Morse, MD. The goal of this study was to answer one simple question: "Are there transformative effects from the near-death experiences that can be documented?"[4] In order to answer that question, Morse and his team administered a variety of psychological/mental health assessment tools to more than four hundred people who'd had near-death experiences, all of whom had various backgrounds and experiences. Morse and his team found a number of changes in people who'd had NDEs. Here are a few of the most amazing findings in the Transformation Study:

- **Decrease in death anxiety:** Near-death experiencers have approximately half the fear of dying as the population that has not had an NDE.
- **Higher zest for living:** This research revealed that those who have near-death experiences have more of the positive traits of type A individuals than those who have not.
- **Higher intelligence:** Those who have NDEs not only feel they have become smarter but seem to have evolved into "higher beings." This is especially evident in children, who seem to mature faster as a result of their brush with death and the spiritual experience it caused.
- **Increase in psychic abilities:** On the average, those in the NDE group had four times as many verifiable psychic experiences as those in the other groups tested.[5]

Although personality change is observed in nearly all of those who have near-death experiences, it happens so often that it is not treated as being "superordinary," only an indication that the superordinary remains an imminent possibility. To me, it's more than that. It's an indicator that all such experiences carry with them the possibility of visible and permanent change and are thus shared experiences on a lesser but more frequent scale.

From Worse to Better

Whether the NDE makes people smarter or not, it certainly initiates a great amount of personal growth in those who have it. And because that personal growth is so transformative in an evident and positive way, I consider these to be shared death experiences.

A startling example of such personal growth from my own counseling practice is a man I'll call Nick. He was a con artist and by his own admission an outright criminal who had done everything from bilking widows to running drugs. Crime had provided a good life for

Nick. He had nice cars, fine clothes, new houses, and no guilt. Then his life changed. He was golfing on a cloudy day when a thunderstorm suddenly developed. Before he could get off the green, he was struck by lightning and "killed." He hovered above his body for a moment and then found himself speeding down a dark tunnel toward a spot of light. He emerged into a bright pastoral setting where he was greeted by relatives and other people who were "glowing like Coleman lanterns."

He met a being of light that he still haltingly describes as God, who graciously led him through a life review. He relived his entire life, not only seeing his actions in three dimensions, but seeing and feeling the effects of his actions on others.

That experience changed Nick. Later, while recovering in the hospital, he felt the full effect of his life review. With the being of light, he had been exposed to pure love. He felt that when he really died, he would have to undergo the life review again, a process that would be very uncomfortable if he failed to learn from his first life review.

"Now," said Nick, "I always live my life knowing that someday I'll have to go through another life review."[6]

From Greed to Kindness

Another person changed dramatically by an NDE was a man I'll call Mark. All his life he was obsessed with money and social position. He had run a medical equipment business, showing more concern with the fast sale and the quick buck than with servicing the equipment after it was sold.

Then, in his midforties, he had a severe heart attack. During this experience, he was reunited with his grandmother and many other relatives and exposed to their pure love.

After he was revived, his perspective on life totally changed. All the things that had driven him before were now much lower on his list of priorities—far below family, friendships, and knowledge.

He told me that while he was "on the other side," he made an agreement with the being of light that he would never again focus so heavily on money but would instead devote himself to being kind.

Ironically, this new attitude has led to greater profits. "I'm nicer to be around," he told me with a grin. "So people want to buy more from me."[7]

Researchers who have interviewed large numbers of NDErs have confirmed the aftereffects of the near-death experience. Some have even alluded to a serenity exuded by so many of these people. It is as though they have looked into the future and know that everything is going to be all right.

Types of Personal Change

I have been able to isolate eight kinds of personal changes that take place in a person undergoing an NDE. These changes are present in all NDErs I have talked to and are so powerful and obvious that their new positivity represents a form of SDE.

Type #1: No Fear of Dying

After the event, NDErs no longer fear death. This means different things to different people. For some, the primary fear is of the terrible pain that they imagine accompanies dying. Others worry about who will take care of their loved ones in their absence. Permanent cessation of consciousness is what frightens still others. People who are controlling and authoritarian fear the loss of control that death brings. Fear of possible damnation frightens many, while some are simply afraid of the unknown.

When NDErs say they have lost their fear of death, they most often mean that they no longer fear the obliteration of consciousness or self. That isn't to say that they want to die anytime soon. What they say is that the experience makes life richer and fuller than ever before. The ones I know want more than ever to continue living. In fact, after their NDE, many feel they are living for the first time. As one person put it:

"After my experience, I realized that by living my entire life in fear of death, I was blocking my appreciation of life."[8]

NDErs who see the review of their life realize that the being of light loves and cares for them. They realize the being is not judgmental but wants them to develop into better people. This helps them eliminate fear and focus instead on becoming loving people.

The being of light most often encountered during an NDE isn't telling them that they have to change. My summation, after hearing hundreds of these cases, is that people change willingly because they are in the presence of pure goodness, which makes them want to change their behavior radically.

One NDEr I spoke to had been a minister of the fire-and-brimstone variety. He preached enthusiastically to his congregation that if they didn't believe the Bible in a certain way, they would be condemned to burn eternally.

When he went through his NDE, he said the being of light told him not to speak to his congregation like this anymore. By speaking of "hellfire and damnation," the being said, he was making the lives of his congregation miserable. When this preacher returned to the pulpit, he did so with a new message, of love, no longer of fear.[9]

Most of the NDErs that I have met are mentally healthier than before their experience. For example, they no longer fear things like loss of control—they no longer want to live their lives from fear, due in part that they know there's an afterlife. And despite their confidence about an afterlife, none are in a particular hurry to "cash in" their current existence. As one NDEr told me, "This doesn't make you want to go out and get run over by a truck to get back 'over there.' I still have a strong instinct to survive."[10]

Type #2: Understanding the Importance of Love

"Have you learned to love?" is a question faced by almost all NDErs when on the other side. Upon their return, most of them say that love is the most important thing in life. Many say it is why we are here and find it the hallmark of happiness and fulfillment, with other values paling beside it.

As you might guess, this revelation radically changes the value structure of most NDErs. Where they may have been bigoted, they now see each individual as a loved person. Where material wealth was the pinnacle of achievement, brotherly love now reigns. As I've been often told in one way or another, "This experience is with you all day, every day. It is imprinted in my mind. When I get angry at somebody or get depressed, my death experience is always there to remind me that the world is beautiful and everybody in it has a purpose."

Type #3: A Sense of Universal Connection

NDErs return with a sense that everything in the universe is connected. This is a difficult concept for them to define, but most have a newfound respect for nature and the world around them.

An eloquent description of this feeling was expressed by an insurance salesman in Georgia who had an NDE during a cardiac arrest when he was sixty-two: "The first thing I saw when I awoke in the hospital was a flower, and I cried. Believe it or not, I had never really seen a flower until I came back from death. . . . I look at a forest or a flower or a bird now and say, 'That is me, part of me.'"[11]

Although the changes you are reading here seem extreme, you will see cases of even greater change in chapter 6, "Spontaneous Muses, Healing, and Skills."

Type #4: An Appreciation of Learning

NDEers also have newfound respect for knowledge. Some say that this was the result of reviewing their lives. The being of light told them that learning doesn't stop when you die and that knowledge is something you can take with you. Others describe an entire realm of the afterlife that is set aside for the passionate pursuit of knowledge.

One woman described this afterlife realm as a big university, where people were involved in deep conversations about the world around them. Another man described this realm as a state of consciousness where whatever you want is available to you. If you think of something you want to learn about, it appears to you and "it is there for you to learn."[12] He said it was almost as though information was available in bundles of thought.

This includes information of any kind. For instance, if I wanted to know what it was like to be the president of the United States, I would need only to wish for the experience and it would be so. The best description I can give is that it would be like becoming Google.

Though most NDErs describe a sense of having information downloaded into their beings only to have most of it disappear when they awaken—"I knew everything in the world, but I didn't bring most of the information with me"—some of them do return with new information, often in the field of arts. One such NDEr who became a successful artist is Moe Hunter from Birmingham, England. Before 2004, he worked at Burger King and had no interest or abilities in art. This all changed when he came down with a deadly form of bacterial meningitis followed by tuberculosis in his brain.

This combination of disease is usually fatal, as it almost was for Hunter. He was in a coma for more than a month, during which his heart stopped. Not long after, he developed water on the brain from infection and had to have a stent put in to drain fluid and reduce pressure inside his skull.

Moe Hunter eventually recovered, and when he did, he was a new man, almost literally. Before the coma, "I couldn't draw, or write creatively, nevermind make all the thing that I have since," he told the local newspaper. Now Hunter does all of those things and more, using recycled materials to build objects from popular culture like Star Wars and Marvel characters, and is a well-known artist on the British Comic Con circuit.[13]

Hunter's story is unusual. Yet for most NDErs short contact with new knowledge is life-changing. It is possible that even this short exposure to universal knowledge gives the NDErs a thirst for knowledge when they return to their bodies, leading them to embark on new careers or to take up serious courses of study.

Type #5: A New Feeling of Control

NDEers become acutely sensitive to the immediate and long-term consequences of their actions. It is the dramatic life review, with its third-person perspective, that allows them to examine their lives objectively.

NDEers tell me that the life review lets them look at their life as though it were a movie on a screen. Frequently, they can feel the emotions associated with the action they are viewing, not only their own emotions but also those of the people around them. They can see seemingly unrelated events become connected and witness their "rights" and "wrongs" with crystal clarity. This experience has taught them that at the end of their life, they will have to be the agent and recipient of their every action.

I have yet to meet a person who has been through this experience who doesn't acknowledge that it has made them more careful in choosing their actions. Their sense of responsibility is a positive one that doesn't manifest itself in guilty apprehension.

A woman who had an NDE on her twenty-third birthday, shortly after finishing her graduate degree, told me:

> The most important thing I learned from this experience was that I am responsible for everything I do. Excuses and avoidance were impossible when I was there reviewing my life. And not only that, I saw that responsibility is not bad in the least, that I can't make excuses or try to put my failings off on somebody else. It's funny, but my failings have become very dear to me in a way, because they are my failings, and darn it, I am going to learn from them, come hell or high water. . . .

It is a real challenge, every day of my life, to know that when I die I am going to have to witness every single action of mine again, only this time actually feeling the effects I've had on others. It sure makes me stop and think. I don't dread it. I relish it.[14]

I have to say that not everyone is so overjoyed about their upcoming life review. I have spoken to many people who are frightened at the thought of reliving their lives. Some of these people were victims of child abuse or perhaps child abusers themselves. I have spoken to convicts and even murderers on visits to prisons who turn pale at the thought of reliving the mistakes they made that brought them to prison in the first place.

I remind those who fear the life review that every life, no matter how good, has its dark spots and, yes, they can be painful to relive.

But a life review has an element that takes the edge off these painful memories. Everyone I have spoken to who has had a life review tells of a being of light that kindly counsels them as the review is taking place. This light being is a gentle counselor, understanding of transgressions and, most of all, loving.

By the end of the life review, the NDEr feels loved and understood. It is this feeling of love that stays with them and creates a visible transformation. It is the visible aspect of the life review that makes it an objectively positive experience that can be shared with observers.

Type #6: Focusing on the Little Things

A "sense of urgency" is a phrase that comes up again and again when talking to NDErs. Frequently, they are referring to the shortness and fragility of life or are expressing a sense of urgency about a world in which vast destructive powers are in the hands of mere humans. Yet rather than focusing on these "big" things in the world, the life review they experience also tends to focus them on many of the "little things" too, like the joy they find in petting their dog or the satisfaction they may feel after taking a long walk, looking at the beauty of nature, enjoying a tasty meal. The obvious message is that we have control over our response to the little things and in that can find a profound appreciation of life. In that, life is lived to the fullest.

To explain how the little things show up in a life review, one of the incidents that came across very powerfully in a woman's life review was a time when she found a little girl lost in a department store. The girl was crying, and the woman sat her up on a counter and talked to her until her mother arrived.

A simple event, to be sure. But it is those kinds of things—the little things you do while not even thinking—that come up in the review as being important.

A common refrain from the being of light is "What was in your heart while this was going on?" as though the being is saying the simple acts of kindness that come from the heart are the ones most important because they are the ones most sincere.

Type #7: A Better-Developed Spiritual Side

An NDE almost always leads to spiritual curiosity. As a result, many NDErs study and accept the spiritual teachings of the great religious thinkers. However, this doesn't mean that they become pillars of the local church. To the contrary, many abandon the dogma of organized religion.

A very succinct and thought-provoking account of this attitude was given to me by a man who had studied at a seminary before his NDE:

> My doctor told me I "died" during the surgery. But I told him that I came to life. I saw in that vision what a stuck-up ass I was with all that theology, looking down on everyone who wasn't a member of my denomination or didn't subscribe to the theological beliefs that I did.

A lot of people I know are going to be surprised when they find out that what is in our heart is more important than our heads.[15]

Type #8: Re-entering the "Real" World

Readjustment to the mundane world is what I call re-entry syndrome. And of course, why shouldn't NDErs have difficulty readjusting? Nearly dying and catching a glimpse of a spiritual paradise only to return to "real life" would require readjustment for most anyone.

Over two thousand years ago, Plato addressed this syndrome in *The Republic*. In that book, he invites us to imagine a subterranean world in which people have been since birth shackled and facing the back wall of a cavern so that they can see only shadows from objects that move in front of the blazing fire behind them.

Suppose—Plato reasons—one of these captives was freed from his bonds and drawn upward, out of the cave entirely and into our world and its beauty. If he was then forced down again into the world of shadows where he tried to describe what he had seen, Plato felt he would be ridiculed and derided by those captives who had never left the cave. In addition, he would now have trouble conforming to the dogma of a now more restrictive world.[16]

It is these problems that I deal with in my psychiatric practice, namely helping people who've had unusual spiritual experiences integrate them into their lives.

For instance, many people won't listen to the NDEr's experience. They are disturbed by the event and perhaps even think that the person is insane. But from the NDEr's perspective, something very important has happened, changing their lives, and no one will listen to them sympathetically. Hence, they simply need someone who understands the experience to listen to them.

Amazingly, NDErs usually receive little support from their spouse or family when it comes to dealing with their experience. Often the marked personality changes that go with the NDE cause tension in the family. After all, it is almost like being married to a different person or being parented by a different person.

As I heard an attendee of a conference say:

> When I "came back," no one knew quite what to make of me. When I had my heart attack, I had been a very driven and angry type A. If things didn't go right for me, I was impossible to live with. That was at home as well as work. If my wife wasn't dressed on time when we had someplace to go, I would blow up and make the rest of the evening miserable for her.
>
> Why she put up with it, I don't know. I guess she grew accustomed to it over the years, though, because after my NDE, she could hardly cope with my mellowness. I didn't yell at her anymore. I didn't push her to do things, or anyone else for that matter. I became the easiest person to live with and the change was almost more than she could bear. It took a lot of patience on my part to keep our marriage together. She kept saying, "You are so different since your heart attack." I think she really wanted to say, "You've gone crazy." [17]

How to Support an NDEr

In the 1990s, I conducted a conference in Seattle on coping with an NDEr that was attended by the general public as well as dozens of medical professionals experienced in dealing with NDErs, including Morse and Paul Perry. During a panel discussion, we came up with guidelines in dealing with the changes that are brought about by NDEs. Here are some of the guidelines that are commonly found to be most helpful in living and loving NDRs.

- **Let NDErs talk freely about their experience.** Listen sympathetically and let them talk about their near-death experience as much as they will. Don't use this occasion to try to alleviate your own worries about life after death or to prove any of your own theories about it. The NDEr has had an intense experience, and they need an open mind to hear the episode as it was.

- **Reassure them that they're not alone.** Tell them that experiences like this are very common and that many others who have had NDEs have grown from the experience.

- **Tell them what the experience is.** Although millions of people have had NDEs, few of them even know what they are called. If the person in your life hasn't really "told themselves" what happened, you can tell them they have had a near-death experience. By having the clinical name for their episode, the NDEr will be better equipped to understand this bewildering and unexpected event.

- **Bring the family into the picture.** The changes NDEs bring to people can be difficult for their families to cope with, even if it's a seemingly "good" change. For example, a parent who may have been a hard-driving type A personality before an NDE may suddenly become a mellow type B after the incident. Such a change can be difficult for family members who are accustomed to the NDEr being demanding and tightly wound. It's important to encourage family dialogue to make sure everyone understands the emotional aspects of the experience.

- **Meet other NDErs.** I like to have new NDErs meet other NDErs. These group sessions are among the most amazing I have ever attended. It is as though they have taken a voyage to another country and are sharing notes. It is wonderful if a physician refers them and keeps the group to about four people who simply talk over the excitement and the problems caused by their NDEs.

- **Have NDErs and their spouses meet other NDErs and their spouses.** To relieve any stresses, I occasionally bring a group of NDErs and their spouses together so they can share with others the effects of the NDE on their family life. They find that other people are having the same challenges that they are, and they

try to learn how to cope with the new person their loved one
has become.

- **Have NDErs read about the experience.** This type of therapy
is called bibliotherapy. Because NDErs are experiencing a spiritual shift, I have found that good media on the subject allows
them the opportunity to review the variety of thought and
experiences at their leisure.[18]

Visible Transformation

When it comes to transformation, it seems that all the studies have been
carried out on those who've had NDEs, not SDEs. Until shared death
experiences get their turn, I think it's still worthwhile to consider this
element a part of SDEs because, in fact, SDEs contain many of the
elements of the NDE. And it's understanding these elements and their
effect on those who have them that gives one a deep and positive transformation about their view of death and life.

A Longer View

An example of this long view comes from a case handled by Morse, of a
woman we'll call Darla, who lived in a rural area of the Midwest in the
1950s. She needed what should have been a simple procedure—to have
her tonsils removed—but in that time and place, there were no hospitals
convenient to her. Instead, she went to a doctor's office, where the physician used ether to put her to sleep on an examining table. Too much of
the anesthetic was used, and Darla's heart stopped.

She went through some of what we now recognize as common
elements of an NDE: going through a tunnel, being drawn to a light,
and feeling at peace. Though she wanted to stay, she remembered her
family and how her death would cause great hardship and sadness. She
returned with a new long view of life:

When I came back to life I knew I had been to heaven. Things were going to be very different for me from then on. I [became] much more easygoing than my sisters. They would get bothered by things like whether they had a date or not but those things never really bothered me.

I think the difference in me was caused by the way I now saw time. It was very different after that experience. I realized that time as we see it on the clock isn't how time really is. What we think of as a long time is really only a fraction of a second. Thinking like that really made me less materialistic.[19]

A New Lease on Life

Here is another case, this from Morse's classic book *Closer to the Light*, which emphasizes the objectivity of transformative NDEs. This is the story of a girl we'll call Annie, a sixteen-year-old with persistent depression. Annie's mother committed suicide; a few years later, Annie decided to follow her mother's lead, not just generally but by using the same method: "I took a handful of barbiturates and swallowed them with vodka, lots of it."[20] Thankfully, not only are pills not always an immediate death sentence but Annie did this while at a party. Though it took the others a while to understand what was happening with her, they eventually did:

A bunch of people panicked. A couple of the boys carried me to the bathroom and one of my girlfriends put her finger in my throat and made me throw up in the bathtub. No one wanted to call the police so they decided to keep me awake and give me a shower. They turned on the shower and kept talking to me.

It took me awhile to realize that I was out of my body and float-ing up to the ceiling. I wasn't alone. There was someone else there, a Guardian Angel or something. We both were made of light. I felt three-dimensional and I seemed to be made of something that wasn't solid, maybe gelatin.

I remember feeling love and peace and also feeling as though I had escaped from all the tension and frustration in my life. I felt kind of enveloped by light. It was a wonderful feeling.

I was very close to my Guardian Angel at this point. I could no longer see my body or anything earthly. I was just there with the angel. The angel didn't speak, but it communicated. I was shown the beauty of my body and of every body. I was told that my body was a gift and I was supposed to take care of it, not kill it. After hearing this, I felt very very ashamed of what I had done and [hoping] that I would live, I began to beg for the light for life. The feeling that came back was the strongest feeling of love I have ever experienced, even more than the feeling of love I have for my own children.[21]

What you have read so far of Annie was not a shared death experience. There is no way to objectively prove that the "Guardian Angel" she encountered truly existed or that she saw herself and the angel as consisting of light. Because nobody but her encountered this entity, it, as well as the out-of-body component, can only be proven to exist in her mind.

However, an objective shared death experience did take place after Annie's NDE. The SDE was that Annie became a different person. She was transformed by what she saw and made a lasting change in her life that *others* could see.

The objective experience took place when Annie told her boyfriend (who'd been cheating on her, which was the final push toward her suicide attempt) to beat it. She stopped drinking and doing drugs and as a result found a new set of friends and began to take school and life more seriously. She no longer dwelled on her mother's suicide, and if she felt herself drifting back to her "old ways" of partying, drinking, and drug use, she remembered the simple advice the angel had given her: that life is a series of trials, none of which are unwinnable.

"Immediately after the experience I felt as though I had been given a mission in life, like I was born to accomplish something," she told Dr. Morse. "The experience gave me an inner energy that has never left me."[22]

Why the Transforming Light Indicates Afterlife

The way things evolved for Darla and Annie is how things evolved for Ebenezer Scrooge, the superstar of transformation who began this chapter. He took his NDE seriously and built on it, and soon, wrote Charles Dickens, "[Scrooge] walked about the streets and watched the people hurrying to and fro, and patted children on the head, and questioned beggars, and looked down into the kitchens of houses, and up to the windows; and found that everything could yield him pleasure. He had never dreamed that any walk—that any thing—could give him so much happiness."[23]

I always assumed, even as a young child, that parts of ourselves are hidden from us. The process of getting to know myself has always seemed to me to be an unfolding of layers upon unknown layers and opening up of concealed and unexpected compartments inside myself. The personal metamorphoses reported by those with near-death experiences can be a source of inspiration to all who know about them. Transformation is a bridge that connects us to a realm beyond physical existence, because in order to get to such a realm, we all obviously have to be transformed, making this yet another reason that suggests, to me, an afterlife realm.

How somebody thinks about life after death depends largely upon their stage of life: Are they older and, therefore, naturally thinking about what may be soon to come? Or has something else happened to bring them to this question? For instance, Plato also observed that people think about life after death when they or a loved one are on the threshold of death itself, which of course is logical.[24] Personally, I have found very few people who become interested in life after death from simple curiosity. So, yes, it does seem to me that there is a strong developmental component in the way we reflect upon life after death.

One striking thing I have noticed is that the older people become, the more likely it is that they will have experienced a sense of crossing over into another realm of existence. This may take place in NDEs (as we have described) or mystical episodes where people seem to be transported into another sphere of reality like out-of-body experiences, which we have also described. These experiences come with a self-certifying sense of super-reality, a hyper-real quality that makes normal reality seem unreal.

It seems to me that as we age, the sense of world after death becomes more natural.

Throughout all this, though, even the brightest and most articulate of people say that language fails them when they try to put their experiences into words, leading me to think that these experiences provoke a change in our language as well as who we are.

5

Reason #4: Terminal Lucidity

Medicine is now confronted with the task of enlarging its function. . . . Physicians must of necessity indulge in philosophy.

—Dana Farnsworth, MD

In my medical career, I've seen many patients seem to resurrect from death. I can safely say that every doctor has. Michael Nahm first named and defined terminal lucidity (LT) as a flash of unmistakable life that takes place shortly before death, sometimes even without any other signs of life, including brain activity, being registered. And because this experience now has a name and definition, it has increasingly become an important subject of consciousness research. TL allows observers to witness both the leaving and the returning of a person's life force, making it also a shared death experience.

A Flash of Life

Completely out of the blue, a patient on the verge of dying springs to life in an amplified form of lucidity. They may acknowledge those at the bedside with a wave or a few quiet words, or they may sit up in bed and engage family members in a regular conversation. Some patients even get up from their deathbed and walk around the room, clearly speaking to stunned members of the family who now think their terminally ill loved one has beaten the odds and will soon be coming home. That is terminal lucidity (TL).

And coming home, sadly, isn't what happens. Always, the person settles back down in their bed and passes away a few hours later, leaving the bystanders filled with questions about how someone so ill could make even a short comeback.

A Brief Glimpse

Among the most extreme examples of terminal lucidity is that of Anna Katharina Ehmer, a twenty-six-year-old German woman in the early 1900s who lived most of her life in a mental institution after a childhood bout of meningitis injured her brain. According to one who attended her, Käthe, as she was called, was "among the patients with the most severe mental disabilities who have ever lived in our institution." She had never spoken, and "we have never seen that she had taken notice of her environment even for a second."[1]

Yet on the day of her death, March 1, 1922, Käthe was lucid. Director Friedrich Happich was called to Käthe's room "by one of our physicians, who is respected both as a scientist and a psychiatrist."[2] She was speaking clearly and sensibly and even sang "The Home of the Soul," a nineteenth-century hymn. Happich wrote:

> Käthe, who had never spoken a single word…sang dying songs to herself. Specifically, she sang over and over again "Where does the soul find its home, its peace? Peace, peace, heavenly peace!" For half an hour she sang. Her face, up to then so stultified, was transfigured and spiritualized. Then, she quietly passed away. Like myself and the nurse who had cared for her, the physician had tears in his eyes.[3]

Here are some observations written by another witness of her death:

> This appeared like a miracle to us. Even bigger, however, was the miracle that Käthe, up to now entirely mute, could suddenly recite

the text of the song clearly and intelligibly. Dr. W. [Wittneben] stated over and over again: "From a medical perspective, I am confronted with a mystery. Käthe has suffered so many severe infections of meningitis, that due to the anatomical changes in the cortical brain tissue, it is not comprehensible how the dying woman could suddenly sing so clearly and intelligibly."[4]

Within a short amount of time, the fully revived—not just resurrected but transformed—Anna Katharina Ehmer was dead.

Happich and Wittneben were in awe of what had taken place and didn't hesitate to speak in public of what they saw. The Nazi party was on the rise at this time and advocated for euthanizing all mental patients in Germany, an idea Happich and Wittneben opposed. They knew the mentally ill had a definable amount of personhood and therefore a right to live. To make their case, Happich and Wittneben began collecting cases of terminal lucidity from the medical literature and witnesses to other such events. One of the case studies presented in defense of the mentally ill was that of a twenty-year-old man who had been in the hospital for fourteen years with "mental deficits" yet who suddenly began to sing. He announced he would soon "go to heaven" and then sang a song and died.[5]

In a memoir of her father, Happich's daughter recalled his opposition to euthanizing the mentally ill during a speech in front of the Working Group for Eugenic Questions in 1932. He said:

I have lived through various virtually shattering experiences, some of which I have experienced together with the chief physician of our institution, Dr. Wittneben. These experiences have shown me that even the most miserable . . . leads a hidden inner life which is just as valuable as my own inner life. It is only the destructed surface that hinders him to show it to the outside. Often in the last hours before death, all pathological obstructions fell away and revealed an inner life of such beauty, that we could only stand in front of it, feeling shaken to the core. For somebody who has witnessed such events, the entire question of legally controlled euthanasia is completely finished.[6]

Wittneben's perspective on Käthe and other such cases of terminal lucidity bolstered that of his colleague. "Who has witnessed something like this ... will realize that we can ultimately not solve the mind-body problem as earthbound humans, but he will also realize that we bear a special responsibility for the souls of the mentally ill who are bound to their frail bodies."[7]

Defined and Recognized

When Käthe lived, her story of TL fit into no known category of experience. Where other medical issues have distinct names that define them—a common cold versus flu, for instance—at that time there was no official name or definition for cases of terminal lucidity to be categorized. Sometimes these cases were called "lightening up before death," which is a phrase used as recently as 2009 to describe TL.[8] In places like Eastern Europe, TL would be recorded in patient records as "madness."[9] In Italy it was sometimes noted as "possession by demons."[10]

In the early days of my medical career, TL was known as a "fey" experience, a definition probably picked up from the Scots, who used that word to describe someone about to die. But fey experiences were not studied by medical doctors in those days, as far I know. They were considered by the status quo to be nothing more than jolts of adrenaline created in anticipation of death. The medical community didn't realize that fey episodes were complex experiences involving things medicine did not like to talk about, like the soul and its survival of bodily death. I soon found out that almost everyone working in the intensive care unit had seen examples of fey experiences. When asked, some even went so far as to admit that they had seen the countenance of the dying "light up" before becoming lucid.

That casual attitude toward an incredible, and somewhat common, experience changed with new knowledge from researchers like Michael Nahm. In 2009, Nahm, now a researcher at the Institute for Frontier Areas of Psychology and Mental Health in Freiburg, Germany, was searching dusty boxes filled with old medical records to find cases like that of Käthe's. Nahm's work provided a major breakthrough by (re)naming and defining terminal lucidity as "the (re-) emergence of normal or unusually enhanced mental abilities in dull, unconscious, or mentally ill patients shortly before death, including considerable elevation of mood and spiritual affectation, or the ability to speak in a previously unusual spiritualized and elated manner."[11] Demonstrating the importance of continuing to search for ever more precise monikers, the TL name is currently evolving to that of *paradoxical lucidity*, possibly to replace the word *terminal* with a more positive descriptor.[12] For the moment, at least, we will be using the name *terminal lucidity* throughout this chapter.

Although Nahm's 2009 study was on people with mental illness and other mental disabilities, TL can also be seen in a variety of people who are near death, regardless of their previous mental state. It's simply clearer to tell the difference between dying and lucid and call that observation objective proof when it is witnessed in people who normally would not be expected to be outwardly lucid.

Like the near-death experience (NDR), TL can now be defined and fit firmly into the world of medicine, especially that of the shared death experience (SDE). In the case of TL, the person being observed may have no brain waves only to suddenly and briefly recover all their faculties. To witness this phenomenon is an SDE. Some say it is like seeing the soul return to the deceased and bring them to life.

Nahm broke the phenomena of TL into four phases, paraphrased here:

- **Beginning:** The patient is assumed to have lost so much cognition that a return of mental capacity is highly unlikely.

- **Return of awareness:** The individual spontaneously and on their own begins to communicate with the healthcare staff or visiting friends or family members.
- **Meaningful communications:** There is meaningful and relevant interaction in which the patient returns to their old self—recalling people, places, and events—which was believed to be gone because of the disease process.
- **Saying farewell and the beginning of the dying process:** The individual says goodbye after their period of lucidity, which may last a few minutes to a few days.[13]

Consciousness beyond Brain Waves

Neurologists wonder how a "non-functioning brain" is able to function without active neurons, and they're putting their money where their curiosity is. Some are doing so because of the connection they hypothesize between TL and other mysteries. Even the National Institute on Aging (NIA), a part of the National Institutes of Health (NIH), has jumped in, funding a variety of studies aimed at discovering the factors that trigger TL, hoping that the answers might result in ways to treat neurological diseases like dementia and Alzheimer's.[14]

Still others who study the brain—the outliers of brain research—are exploring different questions: Is TL a sign that consciousness can return to a dead or dying body? Can consciousness exist without a functional brain? After all, if TL cases are taking place in brains that are no longer considered functional, why then is consciousness able to return? Is consciousness really not dependent upon functional gray matter? Was French philosopher René Descartes correct when he defined consciousness with the phrase, "I think, therefore I am?"[15] And if that's the case, what is consciousness? Does it need a functioning brain to exist? Is TL long-sought evidence of the soul? And if so, what is the nature of the soul? And why does this soul emerge when we die?

Throughout the ages, it has been noted by caregivers that consciousness might not necessarily depend upon a functioning brain. In many cases, it's as though something outside the brain takes over and returns normal consciousness to a person who hasn't had complete consciousness for some time. Let me give you a couple of contemporary examples.

What Brain Tissue?

This case comes from American surgeon Scott Haig in 2007. It deals with a man who fell ill with lung cancer that had metastasized all the way to his brain. An examination shortly before his death showed that there was only a small amount of intact brain tissue. The tumors had not just pushed the tissue aside but destroyed it. In the two weeks before his death, the man increasingly lost his ability to move, and his statements were vague and incoherent. Eventually he lost all ability to speak and move. Tests showed he had no brain waves. However, before his death, as his wife and a nurse reported, he surprisingly regained consciousness. He woke from his coma-like state and spoke for about five minutes quite normally with the attending family members. He said goodbye to them, touched them, and smiled. Then he fell back to the previous state and died within an hour.[16]

Harrowing War Stories

Another contemporary example comes from my coauthor Paul Perry's father, a World War II US Army veteran who suffered a stroke in his speech center that left him with dementia and an inability to speak coherently. Several mini strokes struck in the next few months, leaving him increasingly unable to make sense. That was his life for several weeks. Then, when he seemed to be approaching death, he opened his eyes and began to speak with clarity to his wife and Paul, both of whom were present in the room and had been speaking to one another for some time. Paul wrote down what his father said:

"I'm not afraid to die," he said. "When I was in the army, I thought I was going to die several times. One night I remember being shot at in a little stone house where it was just me holed up with a priest! Bullets were bouncing off the walls, and I was so frightened that I thought my heart was going to stop, it was beating so hard."

From his deathbed, the veteran told several other harrowing war stories, including one of throwing a hand grenade into a foxhole only to have the grenade fail to explode.

"When that happened, I left my body," he told Paul. "And I mean I think I literally left my body. I went to the place where the hand grenades were made and saw someone on the assembly line fail to put the fuse into the one I had thrown."

Paul and his father's wife were amazed that he had even opened his eyes let alone been able to regain his speech. He spoke for a while longer and then said again, "I am not afraid to die. I should have died in the war, so everything since then has been a gift." The father soon fell asleep and later that night he died.

This report is remarkable in a couple of ways: the veteran's speech made a complete recovery. Although he'd been unable to speak coherently for several weeks, he was suddenly able to speak with such clarity that it was as though he'd never had a stroke to begin with. Also, his major stroke and the several mini strokes had left him unable to move his left hand and to walk. Yet shortly before his death, he regained hand function and was actually able to stand, at one time getting up to reenact some of the combat events he talked about. This return of motor and speech functions seemed impossible, not only to the family but to the physician in care, who called this return to functionality "a Lazarus experience."[17]

Materialists vs. Dualists, Again

In the nineteenth century, several philosophers and physicians branched off from material science, which they felt had forced all of science into a mold. They instead began to study "the night side of nature,"[18] known in Victorian times as supernatural phenomena such as ghosts and death experiences. These included intellectual heavy hitters like Descartes, Nicholas Malebranche, Baruch Spinoza, and Gottfried Leibniz, who were all dedicated to solving philosophical questions using the scientific method and mathematical equations. Two of the prime beliefs of these dualists, especially Spinoza, was that human consciousness could not be explained by science and that a soul could operate independent of the brain, though in life they are mostly synchronized, an idea that is now called parallelism. They built this belief largely on events they witnessed at the hour of death, events that would now be known as TL. Some of these doctors were so mystified by the death experiences they witnessed that they went on to search out more patients and through them reach new conclusions about the mind, body, and the soul.[19]

Nahm is most eloquent in describing the questions facing both schools of thought—the materialists (who believe biochemistry explains all thing biological) and the dualists (who believe the body and mind are separate).

> I think if you take everything into account [death] looks very much like a transition. . . . The question is: Can it be biochemically explained? I do have my doubts that it can be explained biochemically. So, yes, I definitely think of death as a transition no matter how you regard it. . . . The afterlife, if it exists, will be very complex and very difficult to understand. The question is: What is the soul, if it exists? Does it persist as an individual? Is it able to dissolve into the Great Whatever? Can it rejoin the Great Consciousness that exists in the background of reality of all existence? Can it pop up again and reincarnate?[20]

One could see how these two groups—the materialists and the dualists—might not get along well, but many of them do. The NIA is now launching a research program on TL in patients with dementia and other diseases leading to cognitive decline and are actively discussing the mechanism and meaning of terminal (or paradoxical) lucidity. The subject seems to reveal both material and mystical feelings and beliefs in the researchers. Further research into this subject, according to the NIA, will likely "expand our current understanding of the nature of personhood and consciousness . . . as well as offer more therapeutic approaches for patients with such declines, give more efficient tactics to caregivers, and hopefully lead to more studies that will allow us to better understand the mechanisms of this intriguing phenomena."[21]

This is a revolutionary message. TL is not only solid evidence that the mind and body can operate separately; it adds to a growing body of evidence that our consciousness can survive bodily death.

A Burst of Speech

Here are case studies gathered by nineteenth-century physician Gotthilf Heinrich Schubert, who blended both lines of thought as part of his research of the soul. Here Schubert discusses a mentally ill woman whose TL happened four weeks before her death:

> Four weeks before her death, she finally recovered from her bad dream that had lasted for 20 years. But those who knew her before her madness [subsided] hardly recognized her in her last state of transformation—so ennobled, enhanced, and elevated were all powers and sensations of her mental nature, so ennobled her articulation. She spoke with distinctness and inner brightness about things, which man learns only rarely to understand superficially in his ordinary state of being. Her story aroused furore. Literate and illiterate, educated and uneducated crowded at this dignified sickbed. All had to confess that even if she would have been taught by the most learned and enlightened men during the time of her illness, her mind could not have been more educated, her knowledge could not have been more substantial and higher

than now, as she seemed to awaken from a long and deep confinement of all powers.[22]

Another of Schubert's case studies ascribes an almost mystical healing power to TL. A deaf-mute man achieved the power of normal hearing and speech before his death. Here is an abbreviated version of this man's case as translated in Nahm's research paper:

> The deaf-mute man was educated in a special school for deaf-mute persons, but still never managed to speak understandably because of an "organic defect" [not specified by Schubert]. Yet, "in the elation of the last hours," he was able to speak comprehensively for the first time in his life.
>
> A sick old man had lied "debilitated and entirely speechless" in his bed for 28 years. On the last day of his life, his awareness and ability to speak suddenly returned after he had a joyful dream in which the end of his suffering was announced.[23]

Given that Schubert was a physician and philosopher who studied the soul, Nahm and myself are left to believe that he felt there was a hidden "inner person"—possibly the soul—that emerged with death that was entirely different from the "outer person" with its conscious ego.[24]

History Continued

After researching several TL cases, a French physician named Alexandre Brierre de Boismont wrote an excellent description of TL, which read, "In certain diseases, the senses acquire an extraordinary delicacy on the approach of death, when the sick person astonishes those about him by the elevation of his thoughts, and the sudden lucidity of a mind which has been obscured during many long years."[25]

American Benjamin Rush, who is credited as the first American author to write on mental illness, also recognized TL, writing that "most of mad people discover greater or less degree of reason in the last days or hours of their lives."[26]

Andrew Marshal went further. The British medical doctor examined and published a number of TL cases as they related to those with mental illness. One of his case studies was a very violent ex-lieutenant of the Royal Navy. He wrote of this patient the following: "The character of his madness was great rage, with loss of memory. . . . His memory so far failed him, that he forgot part of his own name. . . . On the day before his death he was quite rational; asked for a clergyman; seemed attentive to the service of the prayer-book; and said 'he hoped God would have mercy on his soul.'"[27]

Positive Transformation

Witnessing a TL event is a powerful emotional experience, one that brings all of a person's five senses, as defined as long ago as Aristotle, to life.[28] It is also logical that this energy brings other senses to life as well. Since Aristotle's time, science has added other senses: a sense of balance, pain, temperature difference, and direction. In recent years, most scientists now agree on two additional senses: chemical detection (chemoreception) and light detection (photoreception).[29]

After researching such extranormal events as terminal lucidity, near-death experiences, and shared-death experiences, I have a belief that the scientific search for new senses has only begun. As Wilder Penfield, MD, the great neurosurgeon and consciousness researcher, observed: "The brain has not explained the mind fully."[30] Within the context of his quote, I believe senses will be discovered that allow for "paranormal experiences" to be considered perfectly normal. And the discovery of these senses won't necessarily come from the exploration of our gray matter but from the invisible stuff that is the content of the mind.

The events surrounding TL can shock and confuse the observer, making them reconsider their personal beliefs, especially those who believe in a distinct border between life and death. Terminal lucidity imposes a variety of possibilities most have never thought about—the most profound being that consciousness doesn't need a functioning brain to survive. And if that is the case, is this proof that our minds extend beyond our physical selves? What does it mean if dead isn't really dead? Is this event proof of life after death? These are questions that can arise for those who witness such an astounding event.

In examining my own case studies of TL, and in discussing these events with others in my field, I can reasonably determine that the overwhelming number of experiences result in positive transformation for the witnesses. This transformation most likely comes from a number of factors, listed here.

Accepting Death and Embracing Life

TL illustrates that there are unknown and underutilized forces in our lives. These forces are rarely used by the human mind yet are activated during certain intense times, such as death and near death. TL also gives us insight into what our own death will be like and even helps us live life to the fullest. The more we realize that something unknown yet powerful and good happens at the point of death, the more relaxed we will become about our own eventuality. When that happens, we have less fear of death and a greater appetite for life. Here's an example from an observer of a TL:

My son and his wife had been caring for her mother, Jane, who was on a rapid decline from Alzheimer's disease. It was Thanksgiving, and even though she was bedridden, they wanted her there at the dining room table with the entire family. They moved her bed into the dining room and then carried her frail body to the table. It was sad to watch. She didn't seem to know where she was or what was going on.

Everyone carried on as they always did at holiday meals while Jane didn't seem to be awake or aware at all. That all changed toward the end of the meal. She had been uncommunicative for several months. But all of a sudden she became completely coherent. She sat up in bed and demanded food, telling everyone she was famished. Then she engaged in normal conversation, asking her grandchildren questions about school and their social lives.

It was as though the clock had turned back five years and she was her normal self.

Late the next day she fell back to sleep and we couldn't rouse her. We thought she was back with us, but that wasn't the case. She died that night, which felt like a mystery to us.[31]

New Dialogues

Witnessing TL can act as an icebreaker allowing those who remain living to begin new dialogues about death and spirituality. When physicians and other caregivers talk openly and less critically about spiritual experiences, then our institutions are likely to change. For example, when dying patients asks the attending physician what their death might be like, the physician is often at a loss for words. They either fear they will say something that offends the patient due to their spiritual beliefs or they just don't know what to say. "What is death like?" is one of the few questions a patient can't get answered by a physician. Usually, they don't know the answer because it wasn't taught in medical school. I think this will change. It's already more common for medical personnel to take psychological and communication classes on what to say to people in crisis and how to talk about death with the dying and their families.

I have one such example from a man I spoke to at a consciousness conference in Portland, Oregon. He had been an avowed atheist since his teenage years when he became "turned off" by the strict dogma of the church his family made him attend. That changed when his father died.

On his father's last day, the nurse reported a "silent stethoscope" to the doctor, meaning she could not hear a heartbeat. The doctor came into the room and put his stethoscope to the man's chest and then neck and was unable to detect any sign of life. But suddenly the father sprang to life. "He looked at us," the man remembered. "His eyes were wide, and he looked off in the distance. 'I love you,' he said."

The man reported a short and clear conversation with his father, one in which his love of family was expressed loud and clear. Then, grasping his son's hand, the father closed his eyes and in a few minutes was dead.

"My whole attitude changed after that," said the man. "I still felt that religion was man-made dogma and was something I didn't want to follow. But still it was clear that something incomprehensible was going on. Something spiritual. And in its own way, spirituality just doesn't have to be defined by religion. I can't stop talking about what happened when my dad didn't die. And I no longer feel pressured by my sister to follow the 'divine rule' of a church. I believe in the soul because I saw my father return from death. But I keep it simple and believe in my own dogma. To me the only divine rule is what my dad said at the end, 'I love you.'"[32]

Healing Experience

TL can also be a powerful healing experience, especially among those struggling with family dysfunction. End-of-life experiences like TL provide the opportunity to "set things right" in a family. It is common that TL witnesses talk of love being expressed to them by a parent who had never before said "I love you." Frank discussions of past transgressions are often the final subjects between the dying and the living. It is these last-minute conversations that give TL the reputation of being a possible healing event.

Lending credence to the healing power of TL is this story from my coauthor, Paul Perry, who had the opportunity to observe such a TL event in action. Paul was in the hospital visiting his son, who had broken his leg in a motorcycle accident. The first day he visited the hospital, a bevy of nurses wheeled a man into the room directly across the hall. He was asleep when they brought him in, and one of the nurses told Paul that the man had dementia and was very close to death.

The second day Paul came to the hospital, he paid more attention to the man across the hall. The doctor had put him on oxygen, and he just lay there without moving as different members of his family dropped in to see him, tried to strike up a conversation, and then left when no words were exchanged.

The third day brought something quite different as Paul looked in. Around the bed were six family members sitting in chairs, and on the bed was the man with dementia, walking around among the bedsheets like he was onstage, talking to each family member in turn. He was offering remembrances of them, some of which must have been funny because there was occasional laughter from the group.

Paul couldn't hear what the man was saying, but his first thought was that he had just seen a man healed of dementia. When Paul left the hospital, the family members were laughing, crying, hugging, and telling the man that they loved him and were glad he would soon be well.

The fourth day, when Paul arrived, he found the man's room empty. He had died in the middle of the night, a nurse said.

Before Paul left, he ran into some of the family members who had come back to gather the man's belongings. They said something Paul could not have anticipated. The man Paul had seen holding court from the bed had been everyone's least favorite uncle. He had always been dour and self-centered. His most recent behavior, and his last, had been shocking to the family members lucky enough to be there.

"I think he came back to show us how funny and nice he was," said a family member. "It was his gift to us to show us love and attention before he was gone."

Observable Miracles

The story that Paul told me was an observable miracle, an event that can be witnessed but does not have a material explanation.

Peter Fenwick has analyzed hundreds of deathbed experiences in his career. In commentary on TL, Fenwick wrote: "Using our current science, it is difficult to find any specific brain mechanism that would underpin and explain these wonderful spiritual experiences."[33] "However, as we now move towards post-modern science, together with the recognition that as yet neuroscience has no explanation of consciousness (subjective experience), the possibility of transcendent phenomena around the time of death should also be considered."[34]

Remote Terminal Lucidity

TL can happen like a precognitive experience, out of the presence of the person dying. Here is an example of this, from a person who lived in Washington, their ninety-one-year-old ailing mother in Illinois:

> I was asleep and it was early in the morning. The time when you dream vivid dreams but almost never remember them, or recall them for just a few seconds before they dissipate. I was sleeping peacefully when suddenly I saw myself in an airport. I was looking out one of those large windows where the planes can be seen coming and going.
>
> I saw my mother standing midway up the steps of a small passenger plane like the kind that shuttles between neighboring cities. She was looking at me with her face radiant, a glowing smile, relaxed and carefree. She was going someplace wonderful, that was obvious. She was dressed in her typical colors, though I didn't recognize the specific clothes, her handbag by her side, but no suitcases. Wherever she was going, she wasn't coming back.
>
> I stood there, on the other side of the glass, unable to reach her or really communicate.
>
> At first, I thought she was just standing where the sun was shining directly on her face, but realized later that she had an inner radiance that somehow transformed her. It was my mother, yet I sensed an inner spirit that had been released somehow. . . .

I woke up, startled by what I had just envisioned. I was mystified. Never have I had a dream about her, or anyone until now. I would find out later that day that [my] mother was in the hospital and would die a few days later. She was saying goodbye, knowing I would not make it in time to speak to her.[35]

When asked how they would describe and interpret this distant and precognitive TL and its aftereffects, this SDEr said they knew the mother "was full of joy, which was not a common emotion for her. Joyful expectation, she was going somewhere absolutely wonderful and had somehow, already been transformed in the process of getting on that plane, which obviously was a metaphor.... She [was] saying goodbye and telling me that she was finally free of this sickly body."[36]

The dream was confusing at first for the SDEr. But she began to feel that the dream had tapped into her mother's physical and mental state and delivered a message to her daughter in just the way she would have wanted to deliver such news. "It didn't occur to me this was a premonition or her saying goodbye until my sister called later in the day, saying mother was in the hospital for some heart related issues. Still didn't know she was dying until another day or so."

Ultimately, the SDEr said, "It was comforting to know that she might still exist, and I may see her again. It's the only thing that has convinced me thus far of afterlife."[37]

TL's Secret Workings

How does TL work? We don't really know. There is, however, a significant amount of scientific speculation about how this and other such phenomena might work. One theory is that the brain's filtering mechanism, which sorts millions of bits of sensory information every day, opens up at death, allowing the measly trickle of information we usually operate on to instead flood our consciousness and overload our senses. Neurophysiologist John Eccles summed up this theory when he declared, "By far the greater part of the activity in the brain . . . does not reach consciousness at all."[38]

As I have said, after researching such extraordinary events as those that lie within the borders of shared-death experiences, I believe that scientific efforts to understand consciousness have only begun. When it is further understood, many so-called "paranormal experiences" will be considered perfectly normal. And the discovery won't necessarily come from the exploration of the gray matter of our brain but from the invisible stuff that is the content of our mind.

Having a TL Experience

Case studies of terminal lucidity tell only one side of the story, namely that of a person observing another's return to lucidity. Their story is, of course, fascinating, as witnessing any return to life would be.

But what of the person *having* the terminal lucidity experience? What is it like to outlive one's consciousness and re-emerge from the pure darkness of death to the bright light of lucidity? What do they see and think when they make that unexpected return of mental clarity? Do they have a sense of being "out of body"? Do they have a conscious sense of selfhood as they did before their disease or injury took hold? And what is their quality of thought, given that many TL patients are lucid despite a lack of brain waves? Where are those thoughts coming from if not their own brain?

These questions are difficult to answer with thorough medical studies because of the mere difficulty of studying this phenomenon. Dr. Craig Blinderman, director of adult palliative medicine at the Columbia University Medical Center, in a 2018 article in the *New York Times*, summed up the difficulty of "catching dying people at the moment of springing back."[39] Most dying people experiencing TL have things on their mind—like expressing their love to their family—other than describing the sensation of the TL.

Still, there are few cases in medical literature that offer a close look into the inner world of a TL patient. One of those comes from the work of Natasha A. Tassell-Matamua, PhD, and Kate Steadman, noted researchers from New Zealand, who linked an episode of terminal lucidity with a near-death experience.

This case study details the death of a thirty-one-year-old woman, known here as KT, from breast cancer in 1985, as told by her husband. Close friends and family had been called to her side late one morning as she approached the end of her life:

> And then at about 1:30 pm you could see she was starting to pass away . . . Of course KT was lying on the couch, and she was the most peaceful of all of us. She was talking us through it [what was happening to her]. She said she was walking through a tunnel down into the light. She was very peaceful. She was talking along those lines of going to the light and how peaceful it was. And then she appeared to die. And then she woke up maybe half a minute later and said, "There is a heaven. I have been there, and it is beautiful." Then she died.[40]

The researchers asked the husband for his thoughts on his wife's dying process, especially those related to her experience of dying once and returning again to speak and then die again. He felt it was the result of many conversations they'd had about the nature of heaven and a specific request he'd made to her to tell him what heaven was like when she got there. He said, "I would say that when she came back, her life thread or consciousness thread hadn't completely snapped at that time she was going down into that tunnel. I believe before she was completely isolated from . . . before she was isolated from us, she came back before all contact was broken."[41]

As a side note, the researchers mentioned the profound transformation that took place in the husband after witnessing the events surrounding his wife's death. As he told them:

All my life since KT died . . . has been steadily progressing toward the soul. And so I tend to live that life to a degree. I'm not a total soul; there is imperfections in there. But if I don't fix them in this lifetime, hopefully I will fix them next time. . . .

I have been through my wild times. Now, I have polarized the mental times which has taught the soul . . . I study every morning . . . One of them is esoteric psychology. It's wonderful. It's about your growth as a soul and tells you about the personality, which is absolutely distinct from the soul.[42]

What intrigued me most in this paper was the link between the near-death experience and that of terminal lucidity. The woman had an NDE, died, and then returned to have a TL, much the same as some in my own studies.

NDEs Can Precede TL

The notion that a near-death experience might precede terminal lucidity is a challenge to the assumptions that TL might signal the beginning of an NDE and not the end. In researching this question, I found similar cases to the one here. Karlis Osis and Erlendur Haraldsson collected fifty thousand end-of-life experiences, many included in their book *At the Hour of Death*, and found several examples of terminal lucidity springing from NDEs.[43] One was of a man in India who regained consciousness after being pronounced dead and claimed to have surprised his doctors that he had gone to heaven only to be sent back to the living because he had not yet completed his life. Two minutes later, the man died.[44] The fact that he "saw heaven" and had a divine message, as so many NDErs do, told me he'd had an NDE before regaining lucidity and delivering that message to those who had just declared him dead.

Other such cases include the inventor Thomas Edison, who lay dying from complications of diabetes, when he sprang suddenly awake from his coma in a TL fashion and said, "It's beautiful over there."[45]

A few hours later, he died, showing that TL can signal the end of one's life and not the beginning of a near-death experience.

Proof That Can Be Studied

In the end, there is the question of provability: Is there evidence to corroborate that terminal lucidity actually takes place? It's a fair question, and one many witnesses ask. My answer is simple and to the point: *With terminal lucidity, the event is observable.*

Unlike other transcendent experiences, we can see it take place. We can watch as the formerly comatose patient awakens, sometimes as though it is just another day. We can listen to them speak with clarity despite perhaps not having done so in several years. We can feel the (false) sense of joy at thinking that they have somehow beaten an unbeatable disease. And we can experience the deep sadness of being an observer as their mysterious revival reverts into a final unconsciousness rather than a sort of resurrection. Terminal lucidity is objective and observable, which makes it especially unique among other such transcendent experiences.

This observability also makes it easy to study, especially against the background of the materialist's explanation, which can be summed up in the words of Francis Crick, one of the researchers who discovered the workings of DNA, who said, "'You,' your joys and your sorrows, your memories and ambitions, your sense of personal identity and free will, are in fact no more than the behavior of a vast assembly of nerve cells and their associated molecules."[46]

Terminal lucidity flies in the face of that kind of materialistic thinking. It shows objectively that the mind and body sometimes do operate separately. And in doing so, TL reveals a great mystery that surely redefines consciousness. Studying the dying process will certainly make one doubt a purely materialistic world.

As you might imagine, these paranormal events lead to deep emotional responses in the observer. They feel they have experienced something that defies natural laws. No doubt this is frightening to some of the witnesses. However, given the circumstances, they usually come around to seeing these TL experiences as the icing on the cake—just another adventure in a life they now recognize as a big and beautiful mystery.

6

✴

Reason #5: Spontaneous Muses, Healings, and Skills

Our species is the only creative species, and it has only one creative instrument, the individual mind and spirit.

—John Steinbeck

There are many stories of near-death experiences (NDEs) leading to positive life changes. Some experiencers acquire new talents. Others are led to change professions, while others suddenly overcome something like crippling anxiety. And others acquire the life-long help of angelic muses, first introduced to them during their NDE. Because those changes are witnessed by other people, they are shared death experiences (SDEs) too, making this an exciting reason to believe there is an afterlife.

Why these spontaneous improvements take place is not known. Some have speculated that the brain changes due to "neural plasticity," the reorganization of the brain's neuronal connections that sometimes takes place after a stroke or the brain trauma of an accident. Neural plasticity proves to us that the brain is capable of reorganizing or rerouting its neurons to compensate for traumatic damage.[1]

Yet for neural reorganization to be the cause of these spontaneous improvements is most likely impossible. After all, successfully "rewiring" the brain after neurological damage can take substantial rehab, and then effects of original damage most often still remain. There is clearly, to me and a growing number of researchers, something more happening here.

Awaken the Muse

In case ancient history classes have slipped your memory—and this is important to our discussion of SDEs, as you'll soon see—allow me to remind you that the muses of ancient Greece were the nine goddesses of the arts and science: Clio was the goddess of history, Urania of astronomy, Erato of poetry, Terpsichore of dance, and so on.

So many NDEs and SDEs contain a form of the muses, which we now call guardian angels. Sometimes they appear in the form of an ancestor or other passed loved one. Other times they are a being of light that emanates love and guides and inspires the NDEr in their new work or art. They may not always be visible but seem to speak to the NDEr psychically, letting their presence be known that way. I know this may sound like it's past the point of scientific research, so let me give you a couple of examples, the second of which is truly incredible.

The Ghosts of Patton's Past

General George Patton, one of the most prominent generals in American military history, was a firm believer in the paranormal. He had frequent visits from his departed father while on the battlefield. As he told his nephew, Fred Ayer, Jr., in his biography *Before the Colors Fade*: "Father used to come to me in the evenings to my tent and sit down to talk and assure me that I would do all right and act bravely in the battle coming the next day. He was just as real as in his study at home at 'Lake Vineyard.'"[2]

Patton recounted instances where the ghosts of his past took him to a higher level of command. To quote the book:

> Once in France we were pinned down by German fire, especially some heavy machine guns. I was lying flat on my belly and scared to death, hardly daring to lift my head. But finally I did, and looked up to a bank of clouds glowing reddish in the almost setting sun. And then, just as clear as clear can be, I saw their heads, the heads of my

grandfather and his brothers. Their mouths weren't moving; they weren't saying anything to me. But they were looking, looking with not so much in anger as with unhappy scowls. I could read their eyes and they said to me, "Georgie, Georgie, you're a disappointment to us lying low down there. Just remember lots of Pattons have been killed, but there never was one who was a coward."

So I got up, drew my gun, and gave commands. And at the last Colonel George and the others were still there, but smiling. Of course, we won that particular battle.[3]

I don't think this visitation took place as a result of an NDE, but I do believe that it took place as a result of a fear-of-death experience, which are NDE-like experiences that take place at times of great mental and physical stress, like an ultra–panic attack. And, of course, I do believe in muse experiences, which is what I think took place here: a form of NDE in which the mind reaches out for help when the brain can't provide it. Whom does it reach out to? Some might say a guardian angel. Others would say a deep well of energy that is God to some, the Source to others, or something completely undefined.

A Journey of a Lifetime

You can see how materialism and dualism can coexist when you understand there are profound NDEs like that of Rajiv Parti, MD, whose near-death experience took him out of his body and into a world where he is now able to cross the line between materialism and dualism with the help of angelic beings. I spent a week with him, when we were snowed in at my house, during which he told me the whole story.

In 2008, Parti was chief of anesthesiology at Heart Hospital in Bakersfield, California. He derived identity and happiness from his title and the incredible amount of wealth and prestige his job gave him. He lived in a mansion, had several luxury cars, and was able to purchase most any material goods he wanted.

In August of that year, everything changed when he was diagnosed with prostate cancer. Surgery to treat it in that same month led to complications that left him incontinent and in excruciating pain, which forced him back into surgery three times and onto strong pain medication. He soon developed a dependency on the meds, which left him not only addicted but depressed.

In December of that year, he went to UCLA Medical Center for the surgical placement of an artificial urinary sphincter. In the days after this surgery, he became very sick and ran a fever of 104–105 degrees Fahrenheit. He could not urinate, and his pelvic area was red and swollen. Heavy antibiotics were prescribed, but they were slowly overwhelmed by the infection.

Ten days later, on Christmas Eve, Parti was admitted to the emergency ward of the UCLA hospital with a severe infection and fever. Emergency surgery was called for to drain the pelvic region of infection and remove the artificial sphincter. His last waking memory before the anesthetic took hold was the searing pain of a catheter being inserted in him to drain his bladder.

Then he went unconscious.

Although deeply asleep from anesthesia, he was very aware that his consciousness had somehow separated from his body. From a vantage point near the ceiling, he could see the surgeon cut him open and then all the operating room personnel cover their faces as the odor of the pus from his infected abdomen seeped throughout the room. The smell was so bad that a nurse applied generous amounts of eucalyptus-scented water to the surgical masks of everyone performing the operation.

Despite being under anesthesia, Parti's senses became so acute in this out-of-body state that he could hear, see, and smell things inside and outside of the operating room. He even heard the anesthesiologist tell a joke so dirty that the doctor blushed when Parti later repeated it to him in the recovery room.

Still deeply anesthetized, Parti's spirit left the operating room and then the country, drifting toward India where he could hear his mother and sister talking about dinner preparations for that night, finally deciding to have rice, vegetables, yogurt, and legumes. He said that he could see that it was a foggy and extraordinarily frigid night, one that had his mother and sister bundled up to protect themselves from the cold. In one corner of the kitchen a small electric heater glowed, helping to take the edge off the chill.

Rather than being fearful of this experience, Parti became euphoric. People are never far away, he thought. He had the sense of his presence spreading around the world, a feeling of oneness with the world and everyone in it.

Fear found its way into the situation. He had the feeling of being pulled into a bleak darkness, one that was filled with screams and the sounds of fighting.

His awareness drifted from the physical world of the operating room in Los Angeles and the kitchen conversation in India to a place where a great wildfire was raging. He could see lightning in dark clouds and smell the odor of burning meat. He realized that an unseen force was pulling him into hell, leaving him "in the midst of souls who were screaming and suffering."[4]

"What is my karma?"[5] He wondered what he had done in his life or past life to deserve this punishment.

In the middle of this horror, Parti began to have the strong awareness that the life he was living was very materialistic: His life was always about himself. So much so, in fact, that when he met new people, Parti asked himself, "What can I get from this person?"

It was there in hell that the full truth dawned on him: The life he was living on earth was without love. He was not practicing compassion or forgiveness toward himself or others. He had an unsavory tendency to be harsh toward people he perceived to be lower than him in social or professional status. He felt deeply sorry for the lack of kindness in his behavior, wishing he could have done certain things in his life differently. As soon as he had that realization, hell faded away.

The elements of transcendence and transformation are what interest me most in near-death experiences. I rarely meet a person who hasn't been transformed by their NDE. NDErs become kinder, gentler versions of who they were before their NDE. This change is often so complete that they are no longer even recognizable. This was the case with Parti. His brush with death opened an entirely new world to him—an *otherworld*, if you will—one that replaced the materialistic and self-centered world he had so carefully constructed.

There are many parts of Parti's story (now a book, *Dying to Wake Up*) that deeply moved me. One such section was during Parti's NDE when his late father left him with these wonderful words of wisdom: "If you keep your consciousness clear and be truthful to yourself, the Universe and the Divine will take care of you."[6]

When Parti absorbed and understood this, he found himself immersed in a formless, shapeless blue light, where a light being began speaking without words, as though through a gentle whisper in his ear. In the presence of the light being, all the five earthly senses were soaked in love so that Parti was communicating *with* it and *in* it. The closer and more connected he became to the light being, the clearer and more intense the being's message became.

Before parting, Parti was assured by the light being that everything was going to be all right and his path was now going to be as a healer. He was told that he would have to leave anesthesiology and materialism behind. The light being told him psychically: "Now it is time to be healer of the soul, especially of the diseases of soul, of the energy body, addiction, depression, chronic pain, and cancer."[7]

It was for this reason, said the light being, that Parti had to experience the diseases that affected others personally. Without being humbled by pain, he would not be able to have empathy for others.[8]

Help came to Parti through the two angels, Michael and Raphael, who had appeared to him during his NDE.[9] They permeated a high level of consciousness and told Parti that at this high level of consciousness, there was a powerful entity of energy, of pure love, and that this pure love was actually the base reality—the underlying fabric—of everything in the universe. It was the source of all creation, the creative force of the universe.

I believed all of what took place in Parti's near-death experience, but clinically I could only classify it as a subjective experience, one that no one else could witness except Parti. With no objective element in his story, I could not consider it a shared experience.

That all changed when Parti was recovering from his NDE. The angels Michael and Raphael were sent to him by the being of light to interpret his message. The most important part of the being of light's message to Parti was that his days as a physician were over, and from now on, he was to practice a form of medicine called "consciousness-based healing."[10] The problem with this demand was that Parti had no idea what consciousness-based healing was. And he didn't remember much of what the being of light had instructed him to do.

The day before Parti was to lead his first therapy group as a consciousness-based healer, the two angels came to him during meditation. They had shown up before when he was meditating, full of jokes and good humor, but on this day, they were quite serious. They suddenly appeared, made a telepathic transmission of information, and disappeared.

When Parti came out of his meditation, he immediately hurried to his writing desk and jotted down the seven basic truths of consciousness-based healing, which he came to call "The Near-Death Manifesto":

1. Consciousness can exist outside the body.

2. There is life after death.

3. We have past lives, and our experiences therein can shape our current realities.

4. We are all connected to each other because we are all made of the one and same energy that manifests as differentiated matter.

5. Divine beings exist to help and guide us.

6. There are different levels of consciousness.

7. There is one, all-pervading, supreme love and intelligence that is the source of the entire universe, and that love is the supreme source of creation.[11]

The events that took place during Parti's NDE were so extraordinary that he has changed completely the type of medicine he practices, moving from the pharmaceutical-based medicines he believes are responsible for a very high percentage of addictions to a consciousness-based healing to treat "diseases of the soul" using peer-reviewed modalities like yoga, meditation, color/light therapy, massage, and other forms of well-researched approaches that do not cause addiction and lead to overall better health. And the fact that his change is so visible to those who know him makes this case a shared death experience. (And yes, Parti was literally transformed by the light. This is one of those stories that could very well be placed in chapter 4, "The Transforming Light.")

Although each of the cases presented in this chapter have vast differences, they are all spontaneous improvements brought on by death experiences. How this works is unknown, a mystery that has dumbfounded some of the smartest people in the world. And that's okay. Maybe it's not the how or why that matters with shared death experiences but just that they make positive change where it's needed.

As author Frank Herbert wrote in *Dune*, "The mystery of life isn't a problem to solve, but a reality to experience."[12]

Unexplained Healings

Of course, spontaneous change does not always involve guardian angels. There is a healing quality to most shared death experiences that introduces positive changes into a person's physical or mental status. These can heal illnesses, sometimes terminal ones, and even introduce new life-changing skills into a person's life. When spontaneous improvement takes place after an NDE, the improvement is almost immediate, sometimes a change that is so instantaneous it seems miraculous. It's as though a light switch has been turned on.

Healing Power of Grief

Here is one such example from Jeffrey Long's Near-Death Experience Research Foundation (NDERF), the case of Sanna F., a woman who sat at the deathbed of her ninety-one-year-old grandmother and was changed for the better by the experience. Here is her story as she has written it:

> A few days before [Grandmother] died, she told me she saw good spirits around her. The day she died, she was extremely weak and unable to communicate. We tried our best to take care of her at home, but we could all tell she was dealing with pain. . . . She was on her 10th day without eating solid foods. She had bed sores on her back. Many family members were in the room chatting and surrounding her as we sensed the end was near. . . . I noticed she seemed in distress, although she had lost her ability to communicate. . . .
>
> Suddenly, I heard my cousin tell us to look at her eyes. Nanny's eyes were completely open, wider and bluer than ever before and she appeared to be looking straight up at something. Her skin was turning white. It was freakish and startling. I believe I said, "She is seeing God!" My sister and cousin could not move as they just stared in amazement. . . .
>
> Her eyes remained fixed on something above her as though she was receiving a message. Some sort of light (either from within or reflecting from her) was illuminating her eyes. Her upper body seemed to be lifted or elevated, however, I can only recall this because of the angle in which I saw her face. For some reason, I could not

remove my gaze from her face, as though I was instructed to not look away. I got an overwhelming sense that we were in the presence of godliness and although I could not see (with my eyes) what Nanny was looking at, I sensed it was either God, Jesus or an angel. It seemed to have a male persona, was very tall, and gleaming a bright light. I saw this not with my physical eyes, but as a telepathic vision in my mind. I could clearly "see" the base of his long robe touching the ground. He seemed to know everything about Nanny, as though he saw her entire life in front of him. He would be best described as "authority personified." I felt extremely honored to be in his presence. As such, I knelt down in prayer out of respect for both my grandmother's fate and because I was in the presence of this powerful and otherworldly being. . . . I sensed that he was telepathically commanding her to follow him. I felt him say something akin to "Come with me."

Even more shocking, the sense of exhilaration and joy we felt as she was dying and leaving to follow him was overwhelming and far more powerful than anything that can be experienced with a human brain. It was like we briefly tapped into a much broader, unifying consciousness—a sensation which is not replicable. No words can possibly do justice to describe the energy we felt. Oddly, I immediately recognized this feeling. It was home.[13]

The death of Sanna's grandmother was initially hard on her. Something about the experience prevented her from grieving "normally."

"The experience played over and over again in my mind for at least a week straight," she wrote. "I longed for the same sensation of exhilarating energy that I felt when Nanny died."[14]

Then Sanna thought about what had happened, and her feeling took a 180-degree turn.

"Eventually I recognized that it was an honor to have had an SDE," she wrote. "It's wonderful to know that my grandmother is in a better place. In addition, I have had a measurable drop in my heart rate since this event occurred. I was diagnosed with generalized anxiety disorder and have taken medication to treat anxiety in the past. I now feel my anxiety is somehow lifted since this experience. I feel more love for others, including strangers. I don't think I will ever be able to fully process what happened, but I am grateful nonetheless."[15]

Sanna's grandmother died a few years ago. To see if the change in her anxiety level is still improved, Paul and I have communicated with her. When asked if her anxiety has worsened, she offered a resounding no, reporting that her resting heart rate is at least ten beats per minute lower than when she was plagued by chronic anxiety.[16]

"I feel the change goes deeper than just anxiety changes," she wrote to us. "Every thought I have now is much more present than before. I used to focus on the future (e.g. what was coming up on my calendar, what problems were ahead, etc.), which caused me to stress out about things. But ever since my experience, I feel very focused on the 'now.' I recently finished reading Dr. [Bruce] Greyson's book *After* and towards the end he mentioned this phenomenon [being present in the moment] as a common aftereffect. I think this is intrinsically tied to my decreased anxiety and lowered heart rate."[17]

Sanna's story shows that having a shared death experience can quickly and deeply change a person for the better. The change came as a surprise for Sanna. As she put it, "I did not initially think that the experience had much to do with me. At the time it seemed to be entirely about Nanny. It wasn't until a couple weeks later that I started to realize I had lost my anxiety."[18]

Why Sanna's anxiety diminished, she does not know. All she knows is that it was connected to her grandmother's death, and as a result she considers it a parting gift from the family matriarch, one that is a mystery and that she greatly appreciates.

Ignored Miracles

Here is a remarkable story of spontaneous healing collected by Penny Sartori, a surgical nurse in the United Kingdom whose interest in death

studies began in the intensive care ward where she witnessed events surrounding death. It was in the ICU where she collected some of the most
interesting NDEs on record, including this well-attested case:

This man had infantile cerebral palsy. Since birth, he had limped,
and his right hand was permanently in a fist. His ankles often swelled,
and his kidneys did not function properly. None of that caused his
NDE; rather, as an adult, he contracted sepsis after emergency surgery
for colon cancer. Once sepsis has taken hold, it can be fatal—this is why
this story is considered to be an NDE.

Interviewed by Sartori several days after his surgery, which Sartori
participated in, the man told her of leaving his body during the operation and hearing and seeing all that was going on around him. He told
of seeing Sartori pull "something out of my mouth, which looked to me
like a long, pink lollipop, like a long, pink thing on a stick,"[19] which was
later identified as the removal of a surgical sponge. He also witnessed
the surgeon holding something in front of his eyes and saying something like, "There's life in the eye."[20] He told of seeing his late parents in
the operating room and talking to his father "not through words through
my mouth but through my mind."[21]

The man's description of his out-of-body experience (OBE) was
interesting but quite common, as OBE descriptions go. But what happened later, after he was fully awake, was nothing short of a miraculous
healing. When he came to after the near-death experience, which he
had had for a completely different, adult-contracted issue, he could
open his hand for the first time in sixty years! The patient continued to
have normal hand use after his near-death experience.

The patient's sister and a physiotherapist who had been treating
the man for a long time confirmed the previously damaged hand. The
records from the treatment period were checked. The physiotherapist
was of the opinion that the hand could not have been opened without
surgery on the tendons. Not only that but the man's gait also normal-
ized, his ankles no longer swelled as before, and even his kidneys now
worked perfectly.[22]

It's worth pondering this case a moment before moving on. After all, something truly miraculous took place in the course of this man's surgery. For six decades, this man had lived with issues both visible and internal caused by his cerebral palsy. On top of that, he nearly died from emergency surgery for colon cancer and had a profound OBE, indicating that he had probably been very near death.

Yet despite the stress of the near-fatal surgery, and his life leading up to it, he awakened with a reorganized brain and a fully functioning body.

About this case, Sartori said, "There are other cases where people have been healed, but all we know is there is something going on that we can't explain."[23] Of course what Sartori says is true—there are thousands of spontaneous improvements that have been recorded throughout history.

Dreams of the Future

And then there is this short but unique SDE, a promise of a future when a person known here as Eliza thought she had none. First, she underwent an intensive surgery to remove cancer tissue, as well as some other tissue that may also have been afflicted by the dread disease. She underwent several days of 104-degree chemo being flushed through her abdominal cavity. Her dreams during this period were primordial, involving "black tar swamps with monsters that pulled [her] into the dark earth."

Kept barely conscious with morphine, Eliza was "on the fringe of this world, with one foot on the other side."

On the verge of giving up, she felt a hand grasp hers, squeezing gently to get her attention. Then she heard a young man's soft voice calling to her, pleading. "Grandmother," he said.

Eliza opened her eyes to see a handsome young man with dark hair, a person she didn't know.

"You have to stay, Grandmother, because I don't know you yet," he said.

Although she said her memory faded after that, it obviously didn't, not totally. The encounter with the young man stuck with her; in fact, it seemed to be an inspiration to live on.

She told close friends and family about the encounter and how it kept her moving on a path to wellness. One day, to her delight, it appeared to come true. Her son became a father to a baby boy whom she felt would grow up to be the young man she saw while still in the hospital.[24]

Was this SDE a premonition of the future? Only time will tell. But given the way of these experiences, I would put my money on Eliza seeing her grandson grow up to be the same dark-haired boy she saw during her difficult recovery.

Newfound Skills

In addition to healing, previously unknown skills can come to light following an NDE. These often become noticeable following the near-death event when the NDEr becomes focused on a new interest that they previously did not have, as if something within themselves has become activated. Often these skills are artistic in nature. This may also remind you of the section on coming back from an NDE with new knowledge, like was discussed in chapter 4, "The Transforming Light." Moe Hunter, whose story was included there, is a great example of this as he had zero artistic ability before his NDE but came back with a passionate desire to create replicas of objects from pop culture using recycled materials. Others may become painters or writers. Tony Cicoria, MD, in his story, following, became a concert pianist.

A Life-Changing Event

Here's a story of spontaneous improvement that begins with a frightening NDE and moves into a life-changing acquired skill that has brought our subject world fame. Meet Tony Cicoria, an orthopedic surgeon in upstate New York, who was given new abilities—ostensibly thanks to calling his mom from a pay phone while at a family picnic in 1994. As he went to hang up, that was when his life changed:

> With my left hand I pulled the phone hand piece away from my face to hang it up. When it was about a foot away from my face, I heard a deafening crack. Simultaneously I saw a brilliant flash of light exit the phone hand piece I was holding. A powerful bolt of lightning had struck the pavilion, traversed through the phone striking me in the face, as its massive electrical charge raced to ground.
>
> The force of the lightning blast threw my body backwards like a rag doll. Despite the stunning physical trauma, I realized something strange and inexplicable was happening. As my body was blown backwards, I felt "me" move forward instead. Yet I seemed also to stand motionless and bewildered staring at the phone dangling in front of me.[25]

Chaos ensued. Cicoria's mother-in-law screamed from the top of the clubhouse stairs. He looked at her, and she was looking down at his lightning-struck body, but not at him. In short order he realized he was out of his body and invisible, hovering above his mother-in-law. His eyes followed hers, and that was when he saw his motionless body on the ground. *I must be dead*, he thought.

People began to mill around his body. No one seemed to know what to do. Cicoria began yelling instructions, but no one could see or hear him. Finally, a woman took charge. She dropped to the ground and started chest compression.[26]

He turned and ran up the stairs to find his family, and by the time he got to the second floor, his legs had begun to disappear. He was "just a ball of energy and thought,"[27] he said.

In a panic, Cicoria ran through the upstairs wall of the building and fell into a river of "bluish white light," which he described as the most glorious feeling he had ever had in his life. It was "a feeling of absolute love and peace."[28]

Cicoria called this "the God energy," the energy of life that flows through everything and animates the world.[29]

Cicoria visualized a mural that showed the high and low points of his life. It was an illustrated life review that left Cicoria feeling no fear. He was still somehow in the blueish-white river, and he wanted to stay there and go to wherever the river was taking him. But that didn't happen. Like a switch had been thrown, he was back in his body in the regular world, burned from head to one foot where the lightning had exited, and in a world of pain.

Looking up at the woman who had been giving him CPR, he said the first thing that came to his mind. "It's okay," he said. "I'm a doctor."[30]

Cicoria refused to go to the hospital right then, although shortly after the event, he did see his cardiologist and a neurologist, and they gave him a clean bill of health. After about a week of rest and relaxation, he returned to his busy surgical practice. But all was not as usual.[31]

A sudden change had come over him. He felt compelled to listen to classical music. This choice of music surprised Cicoria. Describing himself as "a child of the sixties," he was normally interested only in classic rock.[32] His only exposure to classical music or musical training in general was when he was seven and his mother had forced him to take piano lessons for a year.

Now he went out of his way to listen to classical music, driving more than an hour to Albany, New York, from his home to purchase a CD of Chopin's music, which he played constantly.

Over the course of the following two weeks, he realized that he had to play the piano. Unfortunately, he did not have a piano, nor did he remember anything from his childhood lessons.

Then fate seemed to take over. The family's babysitter approached the doctor with a request. She was moving to another home and asked Cicoria if she could store her piano with them for a year. With the unexpected arrival of the piano, Cicoria purchased beginner books on how to play the piano along with sheet music of Chopin. Pieces of complex music came to him in his dreams, which were no ordinary dreams but felt similar to "an out-of-body experience."[33]

After the self-teaching started, Cicoria had a dream. It was no ordinary dream. It was more like an out-of-body experience, one in which he walked up beside himself and watched as he played in a concert hall. After a couple of these dreams, Cicoria realized that he was not playing Chopin but a composition of his own.

One night after this reoccurring dream, he got out of bed and went to the piano where he tried to re-create the music that he'd played in his dream. No matter how he tried, he could not play the music in his head.

He became fanatical with the music. He was convinced that the only way he had survived the lightning strike was because of music, a belief that led him to pay respect to what he heard by practicing daily from four to six thirty in the morning before going to work for twelve hours at the hospital. Then, after the kids were put to sleep, he would practice more, until he was nodding off. "Somehow, I had deluded myself into thinking the only reason I survived had something to do with this music," he said. "I really became a bit of a fanatic about it."[34]

Over the years and with the help of tutors, including a Julliard-trained pianist, his skills have evolved to the point where he has since played for audiences at what is now the Foothills Performing Arts & Civic Center in Oneonta, New York, and Mozart's house in Vienna, Austria, where he played "The Lightning Sonata," his own composition.[35]

The source of this talent has him baffled. A burn from his face to his foot shows the path of the lightning through his body, but tests to his brain show no changes that might account for his newfound musical abilities.

The famed neurologist and author Oliver Sacks, MD, explored the possible effects of Cicoria's lightning strike and presented a couple of theories. One possibility is that a dormant gene may have been activated by the lightning. Another theory is that he had been rewired by the powerful electric charge. Cicoria wasn't sure "what it all meant."[36] He did know he had acquired a "special gift" and could now tune in to "the music from heaven."[37] That was all the explanation he needed.

How could such a thing happen, especially almost instantly? Events like these are certainly among the greatest mysteries in the world of death studies, if for no other reason than they show that from almost certain death can come a new and improved life.

As Circoria concluded in a medical journal article about his own case, "In my case, being both a physician and scientist, I have approached what I experienced with some trepidation. What is clear to me is that my consciousness survived death and I was able to verify details of my near-death and out-of-body experience that I would have no conceivable way of knowing except through conscious travel of my spiritual self, outside of my body."[38]

In conclusion, Cicoria said, "The gift of life is greater than the sum of its parts and, whatever consciousness is, survives death."[39]

Why Spontaneous Muses, Healings, and Skills Indicate an Afterlife

The spontaneous appearance of a muse or guardian angel who helps guide an NDEr through their whole life or new interests, a sudden miraculous healing, and the acquisition of brand-new or possibly latent talents are all elements of SDEs because the consequences of these are all visible after the NDEr has returned to the living, either immediately or within due course. These may be evident among many individuals who narrowly survived severe life-threatening injuries or illnesses. I have known a number of these survivors over a period of decades. During that time, I was impressed by how their life-changing experiences played out over time. To me, it definitely seems that life transformations brought by near-death experiences are distinctly different from transformations caused by more common worldly life events, such as divorce, natural disasters, or the birth of children.

I think that contact with the divine is what differentiates the changes associated with near-death experiences from those associated with more mundane causes. In some, it does appear that these extraordinary life transformations add weight to the prospect of an afterlife. Near-death experiences are a sort of glimpse of the afterlife, another reason to anticipate a kind and loving life beyond this one. In those that I have spoken to who have faced the near-death events that cause them to meet these guardian angels, miraculously heal, and obtain new talents, though they each have wildly different experiences, I have noticed a singular commonality: They, like other SDErs in this book, are no longer afraid of death. They know that there is something amazing waiting for them after they leave their physical bodies. To me, in combination with their changed lives, this provides further evidence to trust there is life after death.

7

Reason #6: Light, Mist, and Music

When the fog's over and the stars and the moon come out at night it'll be a beautiful sight.

—Jack Kerouac

Back in the early seventies even before *Life After Life* was published, I became a sort of medical confessor for my fellow doctors who had experienced unexplainable events that weren't found in their medical books.

For instance, I first heard of a shared death experience (SDE) from one of my professors of medicine in December 1972. She had heard I was researching paranormal events and told me a precious secret, one she had never told a doctor or medical student. Her mother had collapsed from a heart attack at her home, and this doctor had attempted resuscitation. Her efforts failed, but in the midst of it all, she had an out-of-body experience, rising toward the ceiling. As she turned to look at her mother's comatose body, she saw her mom right next to her, smiling despite the imminent outcome. Then this doctor saw something else, a tear in the universe that seemed to be "pouring light like water" into the room, and with it a number of her mother's deceased friends. As her mother floated toward her friends and joined them on the other side, the light closed down "in an almost spiral fashion like a camera lens, and the light was gone."[1]

Since then, I've heard hundreds of SDE stories, from medical doctors, nurses, individuals at all education levels, and other lines of work. The sheer number of people who have come forward to me, and to my colleagues, with stories of shared death experiences tells me that the stories are underreported.

The same is true of the phenomena we will be investigating in this chapter, the presence of mystical light, mist, and music experienced by onlookers at the time of the event of another person's death. These sub-categories of the SDE phenomenon are witnessed by far more bystanders than have been counted. They go underreported because of their strangeness. If that's lessening even a little now, that certainly used to be the case with near-death experiences (NDEs), as people neglected to report them because doctors called them "bad dreams," hallucinations, or worse—a form of transient mental illness. As a result, the patient felt diminished by their experience and kept it to themselves.

But when a number of people hear or see the same thing at the same time, it deserves special attention. After all, experiencing such things as mystical light, mist, or music while attending the death of a loved one indicates something of a supernatural nature, especially when others are with you and experiencing the same thing. And now, more people are talking about these events, and as they do, their reality is being researched and confirmed.

Elements in Shared Death Experiences

Why do light, mist, and music play such big roles in SDEs? What do witnesses make of this unexpected appearance of these elements at a person's hour of death? Do these take place often? Are they frightening or indicative of a better life to come? And how does science explain these, or do they even try at all?

Before attempting to answer those questions, let's take a look at some case studies of those who have seen these elements in the presence of those who are dying. Keep in mind that the instances quoted here were experienced by well-grounded witnesses, some of them medical professionals who have spent considerable time at deathbeds of patients.

Also of note, you'll find some combination cases, which are rare instances where two or three of these three elements (light, mist, and music) combine into the same case study. For example, in some of the nineteenth-century research, investigators found accounts of ethereal music combining with a light to create almost a light-show effect in the room of a person who was dying. Sometimes the light and the music would persist for some time after the person's passing before fading away. There is even one report included here that combines both light and an OBE.

I will first provide case studies of each of these elements so what we are talking about will be clear. Then I will provide an overall theory of what I—and others—think is happening.

Light

First on the list is the element of light that sometimes can be seen emanating from a dying person or appearing around them, possibly expanding into the room or hovering above the body. Sometimes it appears to be a mist, which is the next element to discuss in this chapter. Interestingly enough, included in the stories here are two instances of a pink mist. Its color can fluctuate depending on the viewer, often appearing as white light but other times as a warm glow.

A Light from Beyond

A prime example of a nurse witnessing the "lighting up" of a patient having a death experience is the nurse of Carl Gustav Jung, the father of American psychology, who wrote of his SDE in his autobiography.

At the beginning of 1944 I broke my foot, and a heart attack followed. In a state of unconsciousness I experienced deliriums and visions which must have begun when I was in imminent danger of death and was given oxygen and camphor. The images were so powerful that I concluded myself that I was close to death. My nurse later told me, "You were as if surrounded by a bright glow!" This was a phenomenon she had sometimes observed in dying people. I was at the extreme limit and do not know whether I was in a dream or in ecstasy.[2]

Those who "see the light" during a death experience—theirs or someone else's—say it is more than just light; it is light with "substance" that "wraps" them in a blanket of love and caring that they have never before felt. Sometimes the light even passes through the bystander.

Here is one such example, this from a home care nurse who said she had attended to about one hundred hospice patients and had never had an experience of light except for the one she describes here.

On the day she [the woman I was caring for] died I spent the morning talking to her, trying to keep her in the now. She responded for a while and then began to fade away. At first her voice became weak and then she became kind of incoherent, saying words that made no sense or not being able to complete sentences. Then she just stopped talking and began to struggle with her breathing.

I sat on the edge of the bed and bent over her. Most patients want someone to be close when they die. I think they get energy from the closeness. This woman was in her nineties. No one ever came to see her, and she didn't seem to care. Her record said her family lived in the Midwest and her husband was long gone.

It was evening and the light in the room was dim, turned way down. Keeping it darker seemed to be comforting, at least for me. She was actively dying so probably knew no difference.

Anyway, I kept leaning over her to listen to her breathing and make sure she was still alive. I did this about five or six times when all of a sudden there was a blast of light that I could not only see but could also feel. It passed through me like a very powerful sound wave and lasted a few seconds, maybe three, for as long as the light was there. Then they both faded away.

I could no longer hear my patient's heartbeat or feel her breath. I thought about a lot of things and right away. First I thought her spirit had passed through me and that maybe it would be bad for my health. I had heard stories of light from other nurses, but never one where the light passed through them. For me it was just a swish that went through my chest. The light seemed to come from the woman as she passed. I was stunned, frightened, and thrilled all at the same time.

Now when I look back on it, I am puzzled. I know what I felt was real. . . . For a long time I felt like I had been chosen to have this happen. Grace from God and all that. And I will say that it changed my life a lot. It made me a better and happier person.[3]

Nine Witnesses

Others have reported the collective perception of entire human shapes leaving the body of the dying, such as in the following example that was related by a friend of vicar Hans Martensen-Larsen in 1930, who described it as follows:

A pious, very dear aunt of mine was dying. What I am about to relate was experienced by nine people, all of whom were present in the room in which she died. When my aunt had breathed her last, and her daughter, holding her hand in hers, said, "Now she has gone over," all of them, her husband, her children, and the servants, saw a figure of light float from the head of the bed through the room toward the window and out through it into the open air.[4]

Revelations in the Light

Most often the light does not emanate from the person dying or even from an angelic being. Nor, for that matter, does it necessarily occur at the moment of death. In the case of this woman, the light that accompanied her sister's death simply filled the bedroom, leaving behind a deep spiritual effect on all who saw it.

> About ten years ago, my very beloved sister was dying of cancer at home in her bedroom. I was present along with my other sister and my brother-in-law. About one week prior to my sister's actual passing, a bright white light engulfed the room. It was a light that we all saw. I felt an intense love and connection with everyone in the room, including other "souls" that were not visible but that we felt the presence of.
>
> For me, I saw nothing except this white light and my ill sister. For many years I thought that this light said to me, "This house, these things, they are not real." I was confused about why those thoughts had come to my mind, but I now realize I was experiencing what my dying sister was experiencing. What a revelation! Words cannot express what impact this experience had on me. This was certainly not something I had ever thought before.[5]

The experience of light has unique characteristics. It sometimes emanates from the dying individual and sometimes seems to take place out of thin air. When that happens, there seems to be no particular source. The room lights up on its own and then fades with or soon after the dying of the person.

The light is considered indescribably beautiful by many who see it. In the next case, the light was so beautiful that to see the artificial light of a light bulb made this nurse ill for a long time after witnessing the glorious light that accompanied the death of her mother.

> My mother's illness came up suddenly and from a state of good health she rapidly went downhill and died a few weeks after diagnosis. Our family was not religious so I had no grounding in things like this.
>
> The light in the room changed. I knew because the light bulbs were the new kind that give off light that looks like it coats things.

When this powerful white light came into the room, I almost got sick to my stomach looking at the light coming from those light bulbs. My first sensation was almost one of nausea at how sickening and artificial they made my mother look. The new light was glorious.

Afterwards, I know for sure that there is life after this. We shed our bodies and go somewhere else. Ever since then, those new ugly light bulbs almost make me sick. I never cared until then, but seeing that ugly light beside that beautiful light turned me off.[6]

Studies show that those who have NDEs report "half of the fear of dying that the normal population does"[7] as a result of exposure to the bright light that often presents itself during the experience. This light has been described as a light with substance and usually includes seeing a glowing being of light that is mostly described as a guardian angel or a deity. Exposure to this light is credited with changes in their personality that last their entire lives. They also report a decreased fear of death and an improvement in general health as a result of exposure to the light. And if that isn't paranormal enough, those who experience the light during NDEs are four times as likely to have verifiable psychic experiences than the general population after the NDE event.[8] The story you have just read above is not an NDE but an SDE, which means that this fascinating research on the effects of the light on the perceiver has not yet been done in SDEs. I hope that this intriguing question inspires my fellow researchers to explore this concept further, and we all can read more about this in the future. More about the transformative aspects of the NDE in chapter 3, "The Transforming Light."

Mist

Similar to light, mist can appear across a whole room or be designated to the body of the dying. A number of those who bear witness to a person's final moments see a mist rising from their body. This is generally defined as being a white or gray or even a pink or greenish haze that is cool to the touch, like fog. Some witnesses report that it dissipates like fog while others have seen it gather into a ball that then slips into an opening in thin air and disappears, leading them to believe that the mist has a destination.

Over the years I have heard many doctors and nurses recount supernatural experiences. It is through them that I came to learn that there is more to a patient's experience than is usually reported in their medical records. It was in my unofficial capacity as "Dr. Death" following the publication of my first book that I heard for the first time one of the most bizarre of these unsolved mysteries—a doctor's encounter with mist.

Seeing Is Believing

Let me call this next person Dr. Smith. He was in his late thirties when we first spoke, but the experience he recounted took place during his residency a few years earlier.

It was a quiet night on the ward, as he told it, and he was sitting in the doctor's lounge chatting with other doctors and studying medical journals. Suddenly the lounge door opened, and a nurse poked her head into the room.

"One of your patients seems to be in distress," she said to Dr. Smith. "Gasping for breath, mumbling, looking wide-eyed—"

She stepped aside midsentence as Dr. Smith got up and went into the hall, and they hurried to the patient's private room. The nurse left and Dr. Smith was alone with the patient. It took a moment for his eyes to adjust to the dimness of the room.

This patient was in her late eighties and a smoker; she had mild heart disease with a severe case of COPD compounded by a worsening cold. She had been hospitalized out of concern for her oxygen levels, which had dropped much lower than during his earlier rounds.

With the twist of a dial, he increased the oxygen coming to her through a nose tube and adjusted the flow of IV fluid. He hoped these adjustments would perk her up, but a check of her heart sounded weak and gave him reason for concern.

"And then, all of a sudden, a mist rose from her body. It was pinkish and hovered like a cloud," he said. "Nothing prepared me for this. You don't find this in medical books, that's for sure."

Dr. Smith watched for a moment until the cloud dissipated. He felt cold and fearful that there had been some kind of mechanical failure with the equipment but was assured later by the facilities department that no such cloud or fog could be emitted by the equipment.

Then he checked the patient's heart and could hear nothing. Her heart monitor was beeping and showing a flat-line EKG.

"And that was it," he said. "What was that cloud all about?"[9]

The Moment Can Be Marked

Interestingly enough, this is another report that includes a pink mist.

This case study of mist being evident at the deathbed comes from a registered nurse named Karen who told her story in the Spokane, Washington, newspaper after a columnist asked readers, "Does anyone really know when the human spirit or soul departs from its physical body?" She attempted to answer the question with an experience of her own:

> More than 20 years ago I had an experience that is still fresh in my mind. I was working in the intensive care unit at [a local hospital], and one of my patients was a young man who had been injured in a car accident. . . . He was on life support. His parents had agreed to organ donation and we were waiting for that process to start. His mother and I stood, early in the morning, on each side of his bed, looking down on this beautiful young man who just appeared to be sleeping. As his chest continued to rise and fall, I felt—rather than saw—an odd change in the quality of light in the room. A pink mist then seemed to manifest over his body, where it hovered for a

moment, then lifted off into the room and faded to nothing. The ventilator continued to push air into his lungs . . . but it seemed as if his body had hollowed out, becoming a flat shell. There is no real scientific proof of a living creature having a soul, but at that moment I felt as if I had just witnessed that soul leaving its body.[10]

Reports of Smoky Haze

There have been numerous reports of mist gathering around the deathbed, yet these reports are often discarded by most in the medical profession as being hallucinations. But not all. Peter Fenwick, MD, a fellow of the Royal College of Psychiatrists in Great Britain and a noted British neuropsychiatrist, discussed the smoke or "grey mist" that leaves the body at death in the book he cowrote with his wife Elizabeth Fenwick, also an end-of-life researcher, in 2008.[11] And in 1970, Robert Crookall, an English psychical researcher, wrote about Dr. R. B. Hout's experience with the mist while observing his aunt's passing:

> My attention was called . . . to something immediately above the physical body, suspended in the atmosphere about two feet above the bed. At first I could distinguish nothing more than a vague outline of a hazy, foglike substance. There seemed to be only a mist held suspended, motionless. But, as I looked, very gradually there grew into my sight a denser, more solid, condensation of this inexplicable vapor. Then I was astonished to see definite outlines presenting themselves, and soon I saw this fog-like substance was assuming a human form.[12]

Mist-ical Experience

Here is the dramatic perception of a mother who saw her son leave his body. Her son passed away shortly after, even though the doctor thought he would live. This took place in Seattle in the 1990s:

I was hysterical. Doctors ran into the room, and I was ushered out while the doctors worked over his body. I could watch through glass windows in the hall as they did their work. I was crying because I expected the worst. Suddenly I saw him fly right out of his body! I could see this misty wisp go right up. He moved around near the ceiling for a few seconds, and then he just disappeared! One of the doctors came out and told me that they had gotten him back, but I knew they hadn't. I told him that I had just seen my boy leave his body, and the doctor asked if I would like to sit down. A few moments later another doctor came out and announced that he had died.[13]

Some See Mist, Some See Nothing

One of the exciting aspects of mist is that usually everyone in the room with the dying person sees it. But there are unique cases involving just one witness within a group, such as this from a person I spoke with at a conference in Europe: "When my mother died, I saw a wisp of smoke coming from her head. It hung there for a moment and then floated to the ceiling, stayed there a moment, and then floated through the ceiling and was gone. My sister was in the room with us and didn't see anything unusual. To this day she doesn't believe me, but I am certain of what I saw."[14]

I have heard similar accounts from others, that they alone witnessed the mist rising from a dying patient while others saw nothing. To confuse matters, the person seeing the mist is often an atheist and does not believe in a soul or anything resembling a soul or, for that matter, anything considered supernatural. Yet they are the one in the room who reports adamantly that a mist appears.

I have no idea why this might take place, only that it does. As a parallel event, let me say that during mass sightings of religious figures, like the visions of the Virgin Mary that took place in Cairo, Egypt, in 1968, it was reported by Harvard professor Otto Meinardus that many who witnessed the visions (there were several over a period of many months) were avowed atheists, while extremely religious people were frustrated to see nothing.[15]

To me accounts like the one from Egypt and many others like it simply add to the mystery of all kinds of visions.

The Psychic Judge

And for good measure, here is another experience of mist at death, this from John Edmonds, Chief Justice of the New York Supreme Court, who investigated mediums with the intent of exposing them as frauds and then became a medium himself, developing psychic abilities that he proudly shared.

In his journal on November 24, 1851, he wrote about witnessing the death of his brother-in-law in which a mist was readily apparent:

> He had breathed his last, and I saw what I supposed was his spirit-body issue from his mortal body in the shape of a cloudy frame, and directly over it, and in the room where it lay, it assumed the human form, but it seemed to have no intelligence. Suddenly it lighted up, was alive and intelligent, and I was impressed that that was caused by the soul's leaving his fleshy body and entering his spiritual body. As soon as that intelligence appeared, he looked around as if somewhat in doubt where he was, but he immediately seemed to recollect that his present condition was not strange to him, and to know from previous instruction that he was in the spirit-world.[16]

Combination Case: Mist and an OBE

This is one of the most unique and powerful SDEs I have ever heard. It contains within it both mist and a profound out-of-body experience, a joint vision by a doctor and a nurse of a woman who had just died in a car accident and was floating in a white cloud over her husband, who was about to have life-saving trauma surgery. Here it is:

Graphic artist Jeff Olsen was in a horrible one-car accident in Utah with his family that led to the death of his wife and one of their two children.

Olsen almost immediately left his body, floating above the car accident in what he called a bubble of light that emanated peace and painlessness. In this bubble with him was his wife, Tamara. He knew she was dead from the accident below, but now, inside the bubble, she spoke to him, insisting that he stay alive to take care of their living son, Spencer, who was crying from pain and fear in the back seat. Olsen's consciousness faded to black.

The next thing Olsen knew, he was in a hospital, still out of his body and roaming the halls, able, he said, to see the entire lives of the people he encountered. Soon he found himself in a surgical suite and there looked down as his body with his legs crushed, his right arm in shreds, and his abdomen a mess beyond his description. "*Is that me?*" he thought. "I couldn't go back to that! Then I remembered what Tamara had said [in the bubble]."[17] Olsen knew he had no choice but to go back. After that, his consciousness faded again, this time into the deep sleep of anesthesia.

One of the first surgeons to work on him was veteran ER doctor Jeff O'Driscoll. He walked into the surgical theater and immediately, even through the chaos of emergency surgery preparation, "sensed a divine presence," he told an interviewer in *Guideposts* magazine. "And then I noticed a light. In it was the form of a woman, floating above the patient's bed. She had flowing, curly blonde hair and was dressed in various shades of white. Her form was almost transparent, and the look on her face was serene. She looked vibrant, otherworldly—I knew innately that this was the man's wife. The divine presence in the room was allowing me to view her eternal soul."[18]

O'Driscoll said he sensed her immense gratitude toward him and the other doctors in the room. She also told him psychically that her husband had to survive to care for their living son.

In another part of the surgical suite was Rachel, an ER nurse who had worked with O'Driscoll for several months. She stepped over to him and grabbed his arm. "Did you see her too?"[19] she asked O'Driscoll. He confirmed that he had seen Olsen's wife too, but when he looked back over the surgical table, Tamara was gone.

Several days later, O'Driscoll and Rachel got together with Olsen in his hospital room where they all shared their stories: Olsen told of his out-of-body experience, and O'Driscoll and Rachel their shared death experience with Tamara, Jeff's glowing wife.

This joint experience brought great closure to Olsen, who was plagued by guilt because of the accident. But now, having heard from his wife when they were in the bubble that he shouldn't feel guilty about the accident, he was now hearing from his first surgeon that she had told him the same thing.

Eighteen surgeries later, Olsen left the hospital and moved in with his brother. One day he received a call from O'Driscoll, who wanted to drop by and see how he was doing. Olsen accepted, and the two spent time talking about the experience that had taken place in the operating room. From that time on, they were fast friends.[20]

Over the years, I have become well acquainted with both Olsen and O'Driscoll. I find them to be very honest and credible people, so I am in no way concerned about what happened here. These events truly happened. And that Tamara made her presence known to her husband, the doctor, and the ER nurse convinces me without a doubt that she was a very powerful spirit who wanted her final wishes to be known among those who could make it happen, down to being able to glow brightly enough to get their attention.

So, my question here isn't *did* it happen, but *how* did it happen? And to that I have no answer, only that it did. That said, I have spoken to scientists who are in different disciplines than I and have heard some believable explanations of why death experiences like these take place, including one from a psychologist, who said, and I quote him from memory, "The laws of physics can change at the extremes of nature. So, if death can be considered an extreme, then all kinds of paranormal experiences can be expected, especially the deeper into death."[21]

Music

The most overriding observations about music are that it seems to emanate from no particular source and no particular direction. It is almost always described as being "heavenly." Sometimes the experiencer describes the music as orchestral, using musical instruments they cannot identify; other times it can be long and sustained notes, and one NDEr described the notes as "so beautiful they cannot be mimicked by anything I know." This same NDEr, who heard the music at the death of his mother, called it "sentient sound, the type of music that made me think it was a living, breathing being."[22] The best description I've heard came from my mentor in this field, Dr. George Ritchie, who declared that the music he heard during his NDE was "more like Beethoven than the Beatles."[23]

Time and again NDErs tell me that just the thought of the music, which always seems to embed its uniqueness into the consciousness of those who hear it, can put them into a "mystical place," while trying to re-create it is a futile exercise. Even the musically inclined who hear it have not, to my knowledge, ever reproduced the sounds, despite what amounts to an obsession in many who continue for years to try. "Still," said another NDEr, "I long for the day when I hear it again."[24]

Mystical Music

Here is a brief case regarding the mystical music from the ground-breaking body of research collected by Edmund Gurney, Frederic W. H. Myers, and Frank Podmore, founders of The Society for Psychical Research in nineteenth-century England.

In 1881, a Mr. L. wrote to Gurney about the death of his mother. He reported that as soon as his mother had died, two women (presumably friends of the deceased) exited the room and heard "low, soft music, exceedingly sweet, as if of three girls' voices."[25] They were under the impression that it came from the street. Two others heard the music from different areas of the house, though Mr. L. himself did not. Then the two women heard the singing again quite strongly as they climbed the stairs back to the room where the deceased still lay. It was only after the event that the four people discussed and realized that they had all heard the very same music and melodic voices. One described the music "as if several voices were singing in perfect unison a most sweet melody, which died away in the distance."[26] Interesting to me are the comments made by the doctor giving the account that he had no belief in the supernatural, yet still offered the facts as they occurred, which are clearly those of a supernatural occurrence.

> I remember the circumstance perfectly. Poor Mrs. L. died on July 28th, 1881. I was sent for at about midnight, and remained until her death at about 2:30 AM. As there was no qualified nurse present, I remained and assisted the friends to "lay out" the body. Four or five of us assisted, and at my request the matron of Mr. L.'s house and a servant went to the kitchen department to find a shutter or flat board upon which to place the body. Soon after their departure, and whilst we were waiting for their return, we distinctly heard a few bars of lovely music—not unlike that from an Æolian harp—which seemed to fill the air for a few seconds. I went to the window and looked out, thinking there must be someone outside, but could see no one, although it was quite light and clear.
>
> Strangely enough, those who went to the kitchen heard the same sounds as they were coming upstairs, quite at the other side of the door. These are the facts, and I think it right to tell you that I have not the slightest belief in the supernatural, Spiritualism, [etc.].[27]

From the Moody Files

Here is a case from my own files, this of a man describing his father's relatively peaceful death from cancer and a musical note that marked the period in which he was dying:

Something strange happened that I still do not understand. The last four hours of his life, I kept hearing a distinct hum or vibration, like a musical note, I had never heard it before or since.

The note was pleasant with no variation, but it felt like music. It was unmistakably music. The note was not coming from my father; it was more like music was coming through him. I felt like he and I were bundled together carrying on our conversation in some other place, kind of between the world. It was plain that he was seeing things that I could not perceive; for example, talking to his mother who had died. The hum was something on the order of a hum in electrical equipment and literally seemed to fill the air with energy. Yet never once did I mention it to anyone else . . . because it was immediately apparent that this was a sound from somewhere else. I was holding his hand when he died, and less than a minute later, this musical note just went silent. I felt at that moment . . . a kind of thread that linked me to the spirit world had been disconnected. I know it has only been temporarily disconnected, though. That music from someplace else assured me there is a life after death, where I will see my mother and father again.[28]

Powerful and Loving Music

And just for good measure, here are two more cases from *Phantasms of the Living*, of those who shared this uniquely powerful music with their loved ones:

In 1870 I lost a dearly loved daughter, 21 years old; she died at noonday, of [an] aneurism. At night, my only other daughter was with me, when all at once . . . we both heard the sweetest of spiritual music, although it seemed so remote, my ears were hurt listening so intently. Till some hours after, my dear girl and I were afraid to inquire of each other had we heard it, for fear we were deluded, but we found both had been so privileged and blessed.[29]

This second case is a puzzling one. It involves two people—one who heard heavenly music, while, at the same time, the other person saw a white figure fly through the room. Here is the evidence provided by each of the percipients. First from Lady C.:

In October, 1879, I was staying at Bishopthorpe, near York, with the Archbishop of York. I was sleeping with Miss Z. T., when I suddenly saw a white figure fly through the room from the door to the window. It was only a shadowy form, and passed in a moment. I felt utterly terrified and called out at once, "Did you see that?" and at the same moment Miss Z. T. exclaimed, "Did you hear that?" Then I said, instantly, "I saw an angel fly through the room," and she said, "I heard an angel singing." We were both very much frightened for a little while, but said nothing about it to any one.[30]

And then Miss T. said:

Late one night, about October 17th, 1879, Lady C. (then Lady K. L.) and I were preparing to go to sleep, after talking some time, when I heard something like very faint music, and seemed to feel what people call "a presence." I put out my hand and touched Lady C., saying, "Did you hear that?" She said, "Oh, don't! Just now I saw something going across the room!" We were both a good deal frightened, and tried to go to sleep as soon as we could. But I remember asking Lady C. exactly what she had seen, and she said, "A sort of white shadow, like a spirit."[31]

This case was found by members of the SRP to be solid proof of a shared experience. In their restrained way of writing they called this case to be "more marked," because

the percept being visual to one person and auditory to the other; while at the same time something of the same idea seems to have been suggested to both. For the purpose in view, the case . . . is, perhaps, stronger than it looks. For the fact that the visual and the auditory experience were both unshared, is a decided indication that they were neither of them due to a real external cause; and if they were hallucinations, then (since no words passed till after both had been experienced) it seems at any rate very possible that one of them produced the other by thought transference."[32]

Combination Case: A Music-and-Light Show

I recall hearing one combination case from a patient who came to get grief counseling. She had spent two days in the hospital room where her husband, under hospice care, was dying from pancreatic cancer. At the end of the second day, as her heavily sedated husband approached death, she noticed a light forming from his chest, which began moving down toward his abdomen. It was daytime and the lights in the room were turned off, emphasizing the gradually increasing brightness of the light, which she described as "brilliant."

With the increasing brightness of the light came a sort of choir music, beautiful singing in words that she could not understand or replicate, although she tried unsuccessfully to do so during our grief therapy session.

This chorale of light and music combined to change this woman's mood. She went from feeling deep sadness over the pending death of her husband to a feeling of deep joy and a sense that this was not the end of life for her husband but the beginning of a "new phase" that would begin for him when he "passed, which [she] no longer saw as death."

Within an hour or so, the line on the heart monitor went flat, and with that the light and music dissipated. Soon a nurse came in to make certain the expected had happened. "I'm sorry," said the nurse. "Your husband has passed away."

Oddly enough, the woman did not come in to see me about grief. Rather she wanted to talk to me about the guilt she felt at not feeling sad at her husband's death.

"A lack of grief is common among those who have had a shared death experience," I told her. "A shared death experience indicates a life after death. With the light and music, you got a glimpse of your husband's future and realized that death is just a phase, a passage into another type of consciousness."

For her, that explained another feeling she had, a common one among my grief patients. "Now I have no fear of death," she said. "I feel left behind."[33]

Why Light, Mist, and Music Indicate an Afterlife

The notion of perceiving mist, light, and/or music at the moment of a person's death is relatively common. According to a study by researchers Peter Fenwick and Sue Brayne, more than 25 percent of interviewed nurses, doctors, and carers working in hospice spoke of having seeing light surround the dying patient.[34] Most of these hospice workers considered these events to be profoundly spiritual, and felt, as one caregiver declared, "There is something transitional going on with the spirit, the mind as well, that it isn't just the physical."[35]

To refer back to the question asked by the columnist in the Spokane newspaper mentioned earlier in this chapter, "Does anyone really know when the human spirit or soul departs from its physical body?" The answer is yes, possibly. Although there has been no serious medical research specifically on this subject of timing, one can extrapolate from bystander observations related to the emission of mist, music, and light from a dying person. The rise of the mist seems to take place as soon as death occurs. It doesn't happen a few minutes later but immediately, as though whatever kept it in the body had broken a bond and the mist was set free. The second and most striking consistency is that the cloud of mist is usually reported as moving to a different place in the room and rushing into something like a portal above the bed. Where that portal leads is yet another mystery.

Another similarity is that the mist is visible and consists of some kind of palpable substance or plasma. I can't speculate on whether the plasma is intelligent, but it does, throughout most of the testimonies, hold as a form and move together. Whether it is intelligent or just has an affinity for itself, I do not know.

I am not aware of any researchers who are exploring the mystery of light, mist, or music. The reason for this lack of attention isn't lack of interest. Peter Fenwick, MD, has done an excellent job of collecting these stories and publishing many of them in journals so other researchers can observe them after they have taken place. But to study the substance that creates the phenomenon hasn't been done yet simply because no one knows when or where these experiences will take place. So to capture, say, the mist, and analyze its content would require medical personnel to carry some kind of capture device that would allow them to suck the mist into a vacuum tube.

It is highly unlikely that any hospital would allow such a device to be mandated let alone that many nurses or doctors would ever use it. They may report SDEs more and more, but they don't necessarily focus their attention on them. After all, such research has already been attempted with out-of-body experiences only to find that the doctors and hospital administrators see no value to their patients in this kind of research and are not cooperative with researchers. Hospitals are very busy institutions and see little value in studying death experiences unless the study involves avoiding death. And that's probably how it should be.

And so, until other methods of research are devised, the mystery of light, mist, and music will remain the mystery it is. Regardless of the lack of methodology for further research (at least for now), quantitatively, the sheer number of these case studies that I've heard and read about are enough for me to believe that they hold significant value in proving that the spirit or soul lives on past the point of bodily death.

8

---✹---

Reason #7: The Psychomanteum

Genius is finding the invisible link between things.

—Vladimir Nabokov

Experiences related to life after death come in and out of fashion. Near-death experiences (NDE), for example, were very familiar in the ancient Greek world. Their familiarity waxed and waned for centuries after that. With the advent of modern resuscitation technology, many more people have survived close calls with death than had formerly. Accordingly, near-death experiences became almost a commonplace phenomenon from the mid-1970s to the present day.

A technique related to the afterlife that was common knowledge around the world for thousands of years until about one hundred years ago has vanished almost entirely. This technique involves using a mirror to ease the conscious mind into a vivid apparitional visit, or a reunion, as it were, with a departed loved one. People gaze into a reflective surface like still water, a crystal, or a mirror—usually a mirror these days because of its convenience—in a darkened room anticipating that their deceased relatives or friends will appear in the reflection.

I've conducted research on this technique and have reported my findings in research articles like the *Journal of Near-Death Studies*.[1] To help support my findings, I quote here from major research that was conducted by Arthur Hastings, professor and director of the William James Center for Consciousness studies in Palo Alto, California. In Hastings's research, one hundred participants were taken through the psychomanteum procedure individually in a three- to four-hour process.

All had lost loved ones and were interested in reducing their grief over the loss.[2] Of the one hundred who participated, sixty-three reported contact with the deceased,[3] and thirty-four reported having mental conversations with the deceased.[4] Tests showed that ninety-two of the participants had a decrease in grief.[5]

Most remarkable to me, within my research, was this: even among my graduate students of psychology and the university professors and psychological colleagues with whom I first tried this technique, there was an overwhelming belief that what they experienced was not a dream-like state but a real event.

One of the professors summed up these early test runs when he had a brief yet poignant conversation with his deceased grandmother. "I saw my grandma, but was it a dream or a figment, or was it real? I don't know."[6]

Enter the Greeks

My research led me through centuries and cultures, through which I discovered that all over the world, in early times and modern, intentionally and by accident, people have discovered that by gazing into a clear depth, they can open a door into a visionary world.

The most successful in this arena were the ancient Greeks. They carried out their mirror gazing in chambers called psychomanteums. These specially devised vision chambers were contained in underground labyrinths called oracles of the dead. These oracles were located all over Greece, and their ruins remain to this day. Their architecture indicates that patients spent several days sleeping and eating in massive dormitories while the dark surroundings cleared their minds of the outside world and gave them sufficient alone time to think about the departed loved one they sought. When they were ready for that moment, a priest would escort them to a large chamber dominated by a polished metal bowl in which was contained a pool of still water. The reflective surface and the shadowy surroundings of the vision chamber would inspire a visionary experience, usually one that allowed them to interact with their desired subject.

The psychomanteums in ancient Greece were large affairs. A researcher of ancient Greek archaeology, Sotiris Dakaris, has shown them to be cave complexes with dormitories and living rooms where clients would stay for weeks in nearly complete darkness preparing for this trip to the other world. Inside these psychomanteums, Dakaris found enormous bronze cauldrons that would be polished to a mirror surface to facilitate an apparitional experience. Spending time in darkness would sensitize them in preparation for the moment they would again be exposed to brighter light and the encounter with the mirror, all in hopes of creating an explosion of imagery.[7]

This technique was amazingly successful, as evidenced by stone tablets dug into the ground like tombstones and carved with notes of thanks to the gods they credited with enabling this incredible experience.

Most famous is an episode of gazing described in *The Odyssey* by Homer. Homer recounted traveling to an oracle of the dead where a number of citizens gazed into a reflective pool of animal blood from which came "the souls of the dead who had passed away," including "young men and brides, old men who had suffered much, and tender maidens to whom sorrow was a new thing; others killed in battle, warriors clad in bloodstained armour."[8]

What Odysseus saw made him "pale with fear" as did the image of his mother, who announced, unbeknownst to him, that she had died of loneliness for her wandering son.[9] "When I heard this I longed to throw my arms round her neck," said Odysseus. "Three times I tried to embrace the ghost, three times it slipt through my hands like a shadow or a dream."[10]

Adventures of the Middle Realm

After my research into the Greeks' oracles, I became fascinated with the possibilities of mirror gazing and began to wonder if I could turn it into a usable science, making it an experience that could be replicated at will and studied in a laboratory setting. I began to think of this practice of meeting with the dead through a reflective surface as the Middle Realm. This has been referred to in many different cultures by a wide variety of names, but essentially, this is a liminal space between this world and the afterlife where the living and the dead may meet.

I found this notion to be very exciting for a number of reasons. First and foremost was that mirror gazing could be a very effective means of grief therapy for patients who were unable to overcome the depression and grief caused by the death of a loved one.

Could a mirror-gazing experience relieve grief in modern times as it did in ancient Greece? Seeing a deceased loved one just one more time could be an important turning point for patients getting past grief and getting on with their lives.

I began to write down other questions I would like answered by launching myself into a study of the unorthodox world of mirror gazing:

Does this explain why so many people see ghosts?

Excellent medical research has shown that as many as one-fourth of Americans have experienced at least once an encounter with someone who had died.[11]

By experiencing apparitions of the deceased, I don't mean just seeing one but also feeling, hearing, or smelling them as well. Such encounters are indications that the memories of our loved ones are deeply embedded in our unconscious minds. It would be a step forward in psychological research if we could all have such an experience at will.

Could mirror gazing make it possible to "see" ghosts in a laboratory setting?

Because experiencing ghosts seems to happen on its own, spontaneously, there is no methodical way of studying this phenomenon. Therefore, the study of ghost experiences is just a study of stories that take place on their own, with no way of controlling when they occur.

But if mirror gazing were a method of inducing ghost experiences, then these experiences could be created in a laboratory setting and studied by scientist. By administering an electroencephalogram (EEG) to subjects, we could observe the type of brain waves one has when, for example, they observe a ghost.

This was an exciting thought for me. Not only could we observe brain physiology that allows this to happen but we could also investigate any direct connections between the brain and a possible afterlife.

Could mirror gazing make it possible to view the unconscious mind?

Since the study of psychology began, researchers like Jung and Freud have insisted that much if not most of what goes on in the human mind takes place in the unconscious. In essence that means who we are and how we react and respond to the world around us is largely invisible and out of our control.

Could mirror gazing make it possible to consciously explore the unconscious, making it visible?

Could mirror gazing make it possible to understand the creative process?

So many writers, artists, scientists, and even business leaders credit the unconscious mind for their creativity. Could the systematic use of mirror gazing overcome blocks to creativity?

Already, I had examined the creative processes of many artists and scientists and found they credited unexplored areas of the brain with many of their greatest works. Salvador Dalí, the surrealist painter, devised methods of wakening himself in the midst of dreams so he could apply their surrealistic qualities to the canvas.[12] Hence his melting clocks were born, as were many of his other bizarre images. And Thomas Edison did the same, using techniques to capture the thoughts that arose during that fugue state between sleep and wakefulness.[13] Studies done by Delphine Oudiette of the Paris Brain Institute have proven these techniques to be effective in solving creative problems.

Could mirror gazing be a way of tapping into hidden creativity inside each of us?

Could a study of mirror gazing be a way to explain humankind's propensity to believe in supernatural forces, or is it a way of actually reaching the realm of the supernatural?

Studying mirror gazing could reveal whether a supernatural realm actually exists. Does mirror gazing open a door into another realm? Is this a door that we could learn to open at will?

After I jotted down those questions, I crafted a statement and goal about the work I was about to do:

> As human beings, we are plagued by fear and anxiety of death.
>
> As a society, we put death in its place, creating cemeteries that keep death out of our view. We have horror films to remind us of the terror in death, but other than that, we don't talk about death very much, except when it is required.
>
> In many ways, these restrictions are aimed at telling us that there is a world of the living and a world of the dead, and one side can never venture into the other.
>
> Yet in my experience, there is a midway zone between the living and the dead.
>
> Without a doubt, there are certain experiences of living consciousness that seem to indicate that we survive death. Near-death experiences are one such phenomenon, as is seeing apparitions of the deceased, leaving one's body, channeling wisdom, and having shamanic voyages. These experiences are seen as a transition between life and death. Because they relate to both and yet neither, they might be called adventures of the Middle Realm, a place where the living transition into a dimension of awareness called life after death.

With all of this in mind, my goal was to explore mirror visions, seeing if they are included in those ways of entering the Middle Realm.

The Psychomanteum and Its Guests

I decided to create a psychomanteum of my own. I didn't need one of the large psychomanteums of ancient times. All I needed was a dark, faintly lit room, a comfortable chair, and a highly polished mirror hung high enough that I could not see myself when I sat down in front of it. The only thing visible would be the clear depth in the mirror as it reflected the faint light behind me, usually a twenty-watt light bulb to provide minimum illumination. In the resources section at the back of the book, I provide instructions for building your own psychomanteum.

The real key to a successful mirror-gazing session was the proper mental state of the client who shared my goal to answer one question: *Can apparitions of deceased loved ones be consistently facilitated in normal, healthy people?*

I devised a set of simple criteria for the test subjects I would assemble:

- They must be mature people interested in human consciousness.
- They must be emotionally stable, inquisitive, and articulate.
- None of the subjects could have emotional or mental disorders.
- None of the subjects could have occult ideologies, since such leanings could complicate the analysis of the results.

With those criteria in mind, I contacted ten subjects and asked if they would like to participate in my Reunions Experiment.

My method of preparing them for the psychomanteum was simple and remains so to this day.

On the appointed day (one patient per day), they arrived, bringing mementos and photo albums of the person they hoped to see. They were dressed in comfortable clothing and had eaten a light breakfast with no caffeine drinks so they could better relax.

We started the mirror sessions with a leisurely walk in the countryside, exploring the person's motivation for attempting to see the departed.

They were told there were no guarantees of seeing their loved ones, but we would try, which removed the pressure to be successful and just let the mirror vision happen, or not.

After the walk, we ate a light lunch of soup and fruit and then discussed in detail the person who had died and the relationship that existed between the two of them.

Usually the subject would bring up touching memories. Oftentimes these memories would receive a boost from the mementos that had been brought and set right between us. One man brought his father's fishing equipment. A woman brought her sister's hat. Another, his father's war medals. All were poignant and tangible reminders of the deceased.

Sometimes I would have the subject lie on a bed. The bed was equipped with speakers, and the music that emanated from them could be felt throughout the body via bone conduction.

These preparatory sessions lasted until dusk. Then, at the mystical hour of sunset, I would escort the subject into the mirror-gazing booth and turn on an electric light that was only as powerful as that of a single candle. There, the subject was told to gaze deeply into the mirror and relax, clearing his or her mind of everything but thoughts of the deceased. The subject could stay in the room as long as they wanted, but they were asked to refrain from wearing a watch so they would not be tempted to glance at the time.

An attendant sat in the next room during the entire session in case any assistance was required. When the subject emerged in approximately an hour, they were encouraged, but not required, to discuss what had happened for as long as they desired. Some of these debriefing sessions went on for longer than an hour. I made it a point never to hurry them. The session was not over until the subject decided it was over. Because not every person discussed or discussed in full what they experienced, when I share my findings later, I sometimes use approximations.

I had some assumptions before starting this research. I expected that only one or two of the subjects would see a dead relative. I suspected that those subjects who experienced an apparition would doubt the reality of what they saw.

The picture that emerged was vastly different. Of the ten pioneers ushered through this process, five had powerful apparitions of dead relatives. And all five believed they had actually seen their departed loved ones and communicated with them.

Throughout the time working on my psychomanteum project, the response of subjects has continued to fascinate me. This was especially true in the beginning when half of the subjects had such powerful experiences that they were certain that what happened to them in the psychomanteum represented real contacts with departed loved ones. Plainly, their experiences boosted their personal confidence in a life beyond physical existence. These responses by high-functioning individuals constitute another reason in favor of anticipating a life hereafter.

Following are a few early cases that illustrate what I mean:

First Psychomanteum Patient

The first official patient who tested the psychomanteum was a woman I'll call Rita. She was one of my graduate students at the time. She was in her forties and was a counselor who had come back for continuing education.

She had come to see her late husband, who had died two years earlier, and she was very enthusiastic about the concept of the psychomanteum. We went through the preparation, and then she went into the chamber where she spent about forty-five minutes in the act of mirror gazing.

She came out with a big smile on her face and a surprise result. Instead of seeing her late husband, it was her father who manifested in the mirror. He first appeared vividly in the mirror, and as their conversation continued, he stepped out of the mirror and into the room, where their conversation continued.

Rita was accepting of the appearance of her father instead of her husband, providing an explanation of what had happened. "I know I came to see my husband, but it was probably more the person I needed to see was my father."

Rita had a lengthy interaction with her father in the chamber and then called me the next day to report that her father appeared to her again at the foot of her bed when she was getting ready to go to sleep.[14]

Naturally, I was surprised at what had happened with Rita. Seeing her father instead of her husband was one surprise. But having him leave the mirror and then show up later that night at the foot of her bed were two others.

In reading ancient accounts of mirror gazing, I became aware that this could happen. But that it happened so soon and vividly was very special.

Parental Counseling

An East Coast surgeon came to see his late mother, to whom he felt he owed a great debt of gratitude for his success. She appeared to him in the mirror where she was sitting on a couch. They had a wordless conversation, one that took place through mental communications.

"Was there any pain when you died?" he asked her.

"None at all," she said. "The transition was easy."

He continued. "What do you think of the woman I am going to marry?"

"She will be a very good choice," she answered, once again wordlessly. "You should continue to work hard at the relationship and not be your old self. Try to be more understanding."

After about ten such questions, the surgeon's mother faded away. It was a very emotional time for the surgeon, who felt he had dipped into a realm that he had only heard about and never truly believed until then.[15]

Like an Old-Time Movie

A man in his late thirties was devastated by the loss of his wife. She had been a severe alcoholic and had drunk herself to death. He was ridden with guilt by her death, feeling that he should have been able to control her drinking.

He told me his story, focusing on his few years with his wife and how he struggled with her drinking habits. By the time he finished his story, he was weeping and deep in grief.

His mood shifted completely after his mirror-gazing session. His late wife had appeared in the mirror on a wooded forest path where they used to take walks. His wife spoke to him openly about her drinking.

"It's not your fault," she said, conveying this message wordlessly. "After a while, I didn't care that I was drinking too much. I had no way of stopping."[16]

About ten years later, he came to visit me. He was happily remarried and thanked me for guiding him through the mirror-gazing session with his late wife, saying it had removed his guilt and changed his life.

Apparition by Proxy

A psychomanteum experience that truly surprises me is one I call an apparition by proxy, in which a client is prepared to see a specific vision and another person sees the apparition instead. These have happened at least six times in my psychomanteum and are always puzzling to me.

The first one of these took place with a woman who drove from Oklahoma to see her son who had died less than a year earlier.

As we were preparing for our session, she mentioned in a bemused fashion that for a long time, she had avoided telling her mother where she was going and why. Her mother was very religious, and to her, the psychomanteum sounded more like a conjuring session than grief treatment. When she finally told her mother why she was driving to Alabama to see me, the mother made it clear that their religion didn't believe in such things as seeing dead relatives even if the procedure was guided by a psychiatrist.

The woman went through preparation for the psychomanteum, but as sometimes happens, she saw nothing. With great disappointment, she packed her car and the next day drove back to Oklahoma.

I thought that would be the last encounter I would have with her, but three days later, I received a call from her. She was laughing as she told her story. Earlier that day, her mother was sitting quietly in the living room when she said her grandson walked into the room and sat across from her. She wasn't alarmed—in fact, she was elated—that the vision her daughter prepared to see was experienced by her.[17]

Varieties of Experience

With results like those, I found this to be an exciting form of grief therapy. Instead of having to talk to a therapist about the loss of a loved one, a person in the psychomanteum now had the opportunity of talking directly to the loved one. But I was overwhelmed by the number of people who wanted to come to what I now called the Theater of the Mind. Thanks to word of mouth, radio shows, conference mentions, and finally a book, people arrived from all over the country and then from all over the world. Soon I was overbooked with people who wanted to see their departed loved ones.

I had clearly underestimated the appeal of the psychomanteum. I began to imagine that my rural Theater of the Mind would be like the ancient Greek oracles. Then, hundreds of people each year were so drawn to see the departed that they traveled to the oracles by foot. They often waited outside the oracles for days, camping in primitive conditions or renting rooms, before being admitted to the heavily populated caves.

I feared that my modern-day oracle would be no different.

Soon the patient load became overwhelming. Because the psycho-manteum was still in its experimental phase, I wanted to manage every aspect of the reunion experience. That meant I had to devote all my energy to only one patient each day, an exhausting prospect. Especially considering most were in a fragile emotional condition in that they were suffering from grief. Sometimes these sessions would go on late into the night and would be followed the next day with another person as emotionally needy as the last. Soon I was on a never-ending treadmill of work, all of which played havoc with my thyroid difficulties, which never seemed to fully go away even with careful administration of medication.

The only thing that kept me going was the case studies. They were a fascinating confirmation of the effectiveness and value of this mod-ernized version of the technique practiced so effectively by the Greeks. In the first few months, I conducted more than one hundred patients through the psychomanteum, a number that stayed steady for some years until I had to reduce my patient load significantly due to exhaus-tion. I still conduct occasional psychomanteum sessions, maybe a dozen a year. Still, despite the reduced workload, I have been able to reach several conclusions about the varieties of experience that are had by patients using this amazing technique.

Not Who They Expected to See

One of the categories that many of these experiences fit into was an encounter with a deceased person other than the one they had intended to see. I figure that about one-fourth of the patients visited with some-one unexpected during their visit. Also, many of these apparitions were not confined to the mirror but came out to be with the person. It was as though the mirror was somewhat of a portal through which the deceased could pass. When this happened, patients often reported being "touched" by the apparition or reported that they could feel their presence.

One example came from a man who prepared all day to see his father, who had died when the subject was only twelve years old. After hours of preparation, the man was surprised to be greeted in the mirror by his business partner, a person he didn't even particularly like. Here is how he recounted events:

> When he came into the apparition booth, I saw him clearly. He was about two feet away from me. I was so surprised I couldn't think what to do. It was him, right there. He was my size, and I saw him from the waist up. He had a full form and was not transparent. He moved around, and when he did, I could see his head and arms move, all in three dimensions.
>
> He was happy to see me. I was amazed, but he didn't seem amazed. He knew what was going on, was my impression. He wanted to reassure me. He was telling me not to worry, that he was fine. I know that his thought was that we would be together again. His wife is dead now too, and he was sending me the thought that she was with him, but for some reason I was not supposed to see her.
>
> I asked him several questions. I wanted to know something about his daughter that had always concerned me. I had kept in touch with three of his children and helped them out. But there was some difficulty with his second daughter. I had reached out to her, but she blamed me to some extent for her father's death. As she grew older, she said [her father] had been worked too hard. So I asked him what to do, and he gave me complete reassurance about what I wanted to know, and it cleared some things up for me.[18]

Without question, this man felt his business partner had come out of the mirror to sit with him. It allowed him to make peace with his partner and "put to rest" his worries about his partner's family.

In the study I conducted in 1992, about 50 percent of my patients reported communicating with the person who appeared in the mirror.[19] Six out of 16 of my patients who successfully saw a person in the mirror said they spoke with the deceased person.[20] I don't mean they heard the thoughts of the deceased, but actually heard their audible voice.

My First Time

So, I'll talk about that now, starting with a little context for where and how else I personally had explored this technique. Over the years, I tried mirror gazing in several different ways and in several different places, including in Greece, where I was privileged to visit some of the major oracle sites. Another time, I did it using a crystal ball under the guidance of William Roll, PhD, the highly respected researcher of unusual phenomena, now late. He kept a crystal ball in his office and one day showed me how he used it to provide needed periods of creativity. And I mirror gazed at home where I invited friends and students to participate in table sessions where we used small candles as background lighting and sometimes several crystal balls, so each person had their own speculum and therefore a private key to their unconscious mind. I had moved to an old mill house deep in the country by then, and the creek that ran next to the house provided a constant sound of natural white noise that inspired relaxation in the participants.

These sessions were helpful for the participants no matter what they were seeking. For some, it was relaxation or a chance to put the stress of the day behind them. For others, it went far deeper. Some found keys to understanding troubled childhoods or difficult relationships.

Others still went to unexpected places, namely connections to departed loved ones, which was rare given the lack of privacy and preparation. These loved ones would appear in the crystal speculum, which could lead to gasps of surprise and an unrequited desire for the departed to stick around a while longer.

It wasn't until I had set up the perfect psychomanteum in my country home that I myself had a mirror-gazing experience that completely floored me. I sought an experience with my grandmother Wattleton on my mother's side. I was alone for the day, so I did a leisurely preparation, bringing out family photo albums of myself as a child with Grandmother Wattleton and other members of the family. My father was in the military when I was a child, which was a source of mental depression for my mother, and I was raised by my grandparents and essentially thought of them as my parents. I missed Grandmother Wattleton immensely and had a great desire to see her again. After several hours of preparation, I got comfortable in the psychomanteum chamber and waited for Grandmother Wattleton to appear.

She did appear to me but only in a flash. She looked happy and many years younger than how I remembered her. I tried to engage her in conversation to no avail. She simply disappeared.

I continued to mirror gaze for some time, hoping she would re-appear, but that didn't happen. I finally left the chamber and went back to the dining room table by the creek. I was testing the psychomanteum on several of my students at the time, and they'd all had great success. Not only had they seen apparitions of their loved one, but they had been able to successfully interact with them, some so extensively that they insisted the encounter had been "the real deal," as one of the subjects put it. *Why didn't I have the same experience?* I wondered.

Later that day, as I sat and read on the couch, my grandmother did appear. But rather than Grandmother Wattleton, it was Grandmother Moody, the one I least favored. She, too, had helped raise me, but her stern manner distanced her from me as a child. In fact, I had been afraid of her.

I had no fear of her now. I was glad she had appeared. Although we had no verbal communications in the time she was there, I felt years of animosity melt away, replaced by the realization that I'd had a spoiled childhood and had expected too much respect from my elderly caretakers. If for no other reason, this first session in my new psychomanteum was a success.[21]

Takeout Visions

I began to call visions like the one I had takeout visions because they were apparitions that took place later, after the patient had left the psycho-manteum. Twenty-five percent of those who came seeking reunions had them after they had left the gazing booth and returned home or to their hotel.[22] One such case came from a well-respected television journalist who had come to see her son who had committed suicide a few years earlier. She saw nothing while in the mirror chamber. Yet several hours later at the hotel, her son appeared. Here is what she had to say:

> I don't know exactly what time it was that I woke up, but when I did, I felt a presence in the room, and there was this young man standing in the room, between the television set and the dresser.
>
> At first he was pretty expressionless, and he was looking at me. I was so frightened my heart was going a hundred miles a minute. I am glad I was in a king-size bed because I think I would have fallen off the bed, I was so scared.
>
> What was going through my mind was, "Oh God, there must be another entrance to the room!" That's how real he was, standing there.
>
> This was no dream. I was wide awake. I saw him clearly, his whole body, except I didn't see his face. I looked at him and he looked at me. I don't know how long it was, but it was long enough for me to be frightened and I don't frighten easily.
>
> But then I realized that I was having an apparition, that this was my son. It didn't look like him at first, but putting everything together, I realized it was him. As a matter of fact, it looked exactly like him as he had looked about ten years earlier.
>
> It became very peaceful after that. I was very assured about my son, that he is okay and that he loves me. This was a turning point for me. It was a wonderful experience.[23]

Visionary Encounters That Seem Real

Over the years, I have put hundreds of people through this procedure and of those, a large number of patients come out of the psychomanteum convinced that the encounter they just had was real.

Here is what one of those patients said: "There is no doubt that the person I saw in the mirror was my mother! . . . However, she looked healthier and happier than she had at the end of her life. Her lips did not move, but she spoke to me, and I clearly heard what she had to say. She said, 'I'm fine.'"[24]

And here is what one other patient said about their real encounter:

I saw many clouds and lights and movements from one side of the mirror to the other. There were lights in the clouds that were changing colors, also. For a moment I thought I was going to see [my husband]. But it didn't happen that way. Instead I suddenly felt this presence. I didn't see him, but I knew he was standing right next to me. Then I heard him speak. He told me, "Go ahead, you are living the right way and you are raising the kids the right way." Then I began to see things . . . I was not frightened at all. One the contrary, I was more relaxed than I have been since he died.[25]

Most interesting to me was the change that came over the people who'd had an apparition experience. All of these patients defined their reunion as being "real," meaning they were not fantasies or dreams.[26] Some recounted being able to smell, hear, even touch their loved one. And what they saw was solid and three dimensional. I often heard from my clients something like "Just like I am sitting here looking at you, I was sitting there with them."

Because their experience was real, the subjects expressed a different outlook on life. As a result of seeing a being they thought was extinguished by death, they became kinder, more understanding, and much less afraid of death.

National Interest

Even the national media became interested in the psychomanteum. Oprah Winfrey sent two of her guests to the psychomanteum to get an objective view of what took place during a session. Oprah seemed shaken at the notion that she was having this story on her show, possibly because she feared a religious backlash. Then the guests she had sent to experience mirror gazing came out of the psychomanteum and told the TV audience that their loved ones had indeed appeared to them. One even had the sensation of someone kneeling next to her as she spoke to a departed loved one. As the guest spoke, she seemed very happy and calm.

"When people come out, a certain peace seems to settle over them," I said to Oprah.

That was more than could be said for Oprah, who was visibly rattled by all that had transpired.

"I have many, many, many questions about this," she said.

I shrugged. "So do I," I said to laughter from the audience.[27]

Comedian Joan Rivers was a different story. She went into the psychomanteum to do a segment for her afternoon talk show. Going in, she was all jokes, which was fine by me. After all, humor was her game, and that day it was all about making fun of the psychomanteum all the way into the chamber.

Her demeanor had completely changed by the time she came out. She was weeping out of control, having carried out a conversation with her late husband, Edgar. She believed her conversation with Edgar had been live and in person and had no question about the authenticity of mirror gazing. She had received information about Edgar's suicide that was new to her, information that filled in blanks about his puzzling death. She wouldn't tell what she had learned, but her parting comment was: "Thanks, Dr. Moody. I really needed that."[28]

Objective Proof?

Grief counseling is at the very heart of what I do. Among the most common requests I have from the grief-stricken seems to be an impossible one: to have just five more minutes with the departed loved one. I have tried to grant that wish by following instructions from an ancient form of grief therapy, and most of the time I feel I have successfully fulfilled that wish.

I have never declared that these events are "real." I've never said that the dead return. But I have quoted the people who have these experiences, the ones who say their visionary apparitions are truly a loved one who has shown up to provide grief support.

I admit freely that I have no idea what takes place in the mirror or what it is that some say comes out of the mirror. Is it a figment of the mind? A vivid dream? A different reality tapped into by a simple process used successfully down through history? I just don't know.

I do know that most of those who go through mirror-gazing sessions have great belief in what has taken place, as seen from my research statistics:

- **About 25 percent of subjects encounter a deceased person other than the one they planned to contact.**[29] Why this takes place, I don't know, but more than one subject who has had this happen said the person they came to see was not the person they needed to see, though they were pleased with the alternate contact.

- **About 10 percent of the subjects report that an apparition seems to come out of the mirror and sometimes touch the subject**[30]—**a hand placed on their hand, perhaps, or even a loving kiss.** An extreme example of this was a woman who came to see her deceased son who, she declared, picked her up and hugged her before he left.

- **About half of the subjects hold conversations with the apparition, and these conversations are often mental with no spoken words exchanged.**[31] These are psychic communications that seem strange at first but quickly feel normal as the conversation progresses.

- **In about 25 percent of the cases, the apparition was not encountered in the mirror chamber but in another place,**

usually within twenty-four hours.[32] These delayed encounters usually take place in a meditative setting—during the solitude of a long walk, watching television, preparing for bed, enjoying a good book at home, to name just a few possible situations. Sometimes encounters take place repeatedly, but usually not more than two or three times.

- **Almost all the subjects judged the reunion to be real, and not a dream or fantasy.**[33] In describing his experience, one man said, "It was as real as running into my father on a city street."
- **Almost all the subjects were positively affected by the apparitional experience and changed their view of life and the afterlife in ways they found positive.** With most cases, I find these changes to be similar to those experienced after one has an NDE. Their fear of death abates, and they become more positive about life in general.[34]

Even though I had witnessed their impressions of what they said, saw, and felt, I could not prove that the experience was real, not in an objective way. I knew that having such an experience is subjective because only the person who experiences it knows it.

But then that changed—and changed profoundly. As a result of three photographs and two witnesses, I suddenly had material evidence that proved the reunions were real—not fantasies, not dreams—but real encounters with departed loved ones. Here is the case that changed it all for me.

A Black Swan Case

In 2011, a woman arrived from South America in her private jet with the intent of communicating with her daughter, a young lady who had passed away from cancer in North Carolina. With the woman was her sister and her husband, a wealthy businessman.

Rather than follow the procedure I had prescribed and rest in the hotel before coming to the psychomanteum, she and her sister came immediately from the plane with no rest. She was tired from the long flight yet did not want to go through the lengthy procedure that would prepare her for a successful experience. Rather, she demanded a "short course" that would amount to me talking to her for an hour or so about her daughter and the depth of her grief. She showed me a few photographs of the daughter and offered a number of stories that were dear to her. The sister pitched in with memories too, but despite the information we covered, the mother seemed very tired and anxious, and I didn't expect her to have a very successful experience in the psychomanteum.

She went into the mirror-gazing room, and in about an hour and a half, she came out disappointed. She'd had no experience and saw no reason to carry on further with the session.

The two women returned to the hotel in the early afternoon and promised to come back the next day after getting some sleep. When they got to their room, they settled on their beds and began talking about the young girl they had come to see.

About three thirty in the afternoon, according to the timestamp on one of the photographs, three orbs about the shape and size of large beachballs appeared in different parts of the room. They were clear, and the other side of the room could be seen through them.

Neither of the sisters seemed surprised or rattled by the appearance of the floating orbs. Rather, they were intrigued. The sister snapped three photos of the orbs and put her iPhone down. The woman who came to see her daughter began talking to the closest orb, according to her sister, and through it was somehow talking to her daughter! Their conversation was satisfying and tearful, according to what was told to my wife and me by the sister.

And then that was it. After several minutes, the orbs faded away, and the two women were left alone in the room.

At this point, I want to say that I am not an expert in photo analysis, nor was I there to see these orbs manifest in the room or to experience what the mother heard and saw emanating from the three orbs that appeared in broad daylight.

But I do know that the orbs were photographed and that they likely were not "lens flares," given that the orbs were photographed in different parts of the room yet stayed consistent in size and appearance. And I know that the woman who came to have a visitation did so through the orbs that appeared and that—most importantly—she was deeply moved by and satisfied with what took place that afternoon.

The next day the woman chose not to return to the psychomanteum. The sister contacted my wife and said the connection the woman had with the daughter was a powerful one and she didn't feel as though more attempts would be necessary.[35]

Does this case answer the question of whether these encounters are real and observable by others? In other words, can I safely say that objective evidence has been found proving that mirror gazing can result in a real encounter with a loved one? In the one case presented here, I can say yes, and I will add that if there is one such case with objective proof, then there are several others, certainly enough evidence to say that psychomanteum experiences can now be considered objectively proven events.

In essence, this case study is the black swan theory of psychomanteum experiences. That theory sprang from the belief by zoologists that all swans were white. But they weren't. Dutch explorer Willem de Vlamingh began an exploration of Australia in 1697 and became the first European to see black swans.[36] With that discovery came a new scientific caveat—the black swan theory—in which it only takes the discovery of one black swan to prove that not all swans are white. Or, in the case of the psychomanteum, it takes only one provable encounter in which two or more people see the encounter to show that it can happen again and again.

It is only fitting—and ironic—that I include a quote about what is now known as the black swan theory originally postulated by David Hume, one of philosophy's great cynics regarding the afterlife. Nassim Taleb took Hume's and other philosophers' ideas around the black swan theory further in his book *Fooled by Randomness* that applies greatly to the entirety of this book, to its case studies, to the researchers who collect and study them, and to the study of the afterlife in general. Taleb relates Hume's assertion, "No amount of observations of white swans can allow the inference that all swans are white, but the observation of a single black swan is sufficient to refute that conclusion."[37]

Why the Psychomanteum Indicates an Afterlife

The practice of reaching departed loved ones was widely used by the Greeks. It was also widely used in medieval times for the same reason, especially during times of plague. Its use to seek out the dead was widely known in nineteenth-century Great Britain and America when both cultures developed an appetite for the research on the subject being done by organized groups like the Society for Psychical Research. Mirror gazing was among the practices carried out in these churches, many of which were attended by the celebrities of the day. Psychologist William James carried out spiritualist practices, as did evolutionary biologist Alfred Russel Wallace. Marie Curie and husband Pierre, pioneers in the study of radioactivity, could be found in spiritualist churches too, clearly interested in the possibility of interacting with other invisible forces. Other famous dabblers in spiritual practices like mirror gazing included Mark Twain, Frederick Douglas, and Queen Victoria.

This interest carried over to the twentieth century when the horrors of World War I robbed millions of families of their beloved sons. For the parents of the dead soldiers in that war, mirror gazing became a spiritual practice grounded in people's grief over lost loved ones and their longing to communicate with the departed.

Images of someone gazing into a mirror by candlelight and seeing spirits of the dead were commonplace in the early part of the twentieth century. I've amassed a collection of these images and found plenty of them on postcards and a few on advertising cards that businesses distributed. None of the postcards I collected had postmarks after 1915.

That gap in mirror gazing media makes me wonder whether the advent of radio and then television extinguished this ancient practice.

Whatever the cause, what was common practice about a century ago is today highly counterintuitive. However, evoking the deceased with mirror gazing is making a comeback, this time as an approved method of treating grief in the school of transpersonal psychology.

This means, of course, that further research is required to show genuine contact with the deceased. I look forward to that. But for me, the woman with the orb photos is enough to indicate objectively the reality of an afterlife. I turn the subject of mirror gazing over to other researchers to find more proof in this area of study.

Conclusion

———————— ✴ ————————

True skepticism reveals the truth.

—Raymond Moody, MD, PhD

This book grew from sixty years of interviews, observations, research, personal experiences, and reflections on perhaps the biggest mystery of human existence: Do all these extraordinary and inspiring human experiences add up to proof of a life beyond death?

I can answer that question in the positive. Yes, they do. But to understand why requires us to look at three importantly different levels of the question.

First and foremost is the level of professional ethics.

Second, there is the purely personal level of what I, Raymond Moody, happen to think in answering this question.

Third, there is what *proof* is in the first place.

Let's consider each of these in order.

Ethics: Value to the Grieved

As a doctor as well as a human being, I know that professional ethics has to be the first concern of any attempt to gather and propose rational proof of life after death. Plato pointed out that it is impossible to isolate rational inquiry into the afterlife from the complex dealings and emotions of consolation.[1]

That is, questions of the afterlife present themselves to people naturally, at certain predictable and crucial phases in their psychological and spiritual development. Grief over the loss of a loved one to death is probably the most familiar example of such a developmental phase. Grieving people may reach out for assurance that their deceased loved ones are all right and that they will someday be reunited.

Personal: How Do I Feel about the Question?

Positive statements about the prospect of an afterlife may well console and comfort people who are acutely grieving. When the people making the positive statements have doctoral degrees attached to their names, the effect of the positive statements might be that much stronger. Now, suppose some professionally credentialed individual or organization were to come right out and claim to have proven life after death. That claim would no doubt lift the mood and assuage the distress of many people who were mourning.

Suppose further that a year or two later an irreparable flaw in the original claim were to come to light that would lead to a retraction. Now imagine that scenario from the perspective of someone who took deep consolation from that claim. They might well be plunged back into the depths of their despair on the news that the positive statement had been wrong all along. In addition, they might rightfully be irked at the doctor or doctors or organization behind what turned out to be a false statement.

My point is it's wrong to play around with the powerful word *proof* when it comes to such an emotionally weighted human question as life after death.

That said, what about experiences like those gathered in this book? Can they be worked into a proof of life after death that almost anyone, including non-experts, can understand for themselves? Here, my answer is positive. After sixty years of investigating the question like a detective, accumulating facts, circumstances, and raw exposure to those who have had very dramatic death experiences, I am unable to think of any plausible alternatives other than to say, "Our consciousness persists in another framework of reality after our physical bodies die." Yes, I am forced to say that even though I still stammer in incomprehension when I say it. I have not yet fully internalized the idea that there is an afterlife, even though circumstances compel me to say that yes, I definitely think there is a life after life.

For instance, I have numerous medical doctor friends who were transformed by personal near-death experiences. Unanimously, these doctors tell me not only that their death experiences were real but that their experiences were *hyper* real, far more real in fact than ordinary waking reality. Then I ask myself, *Would I trust these dear friends' medical judgment if I were to become ill or injured?* And in every case, my answer is a resounding *Yes!*

Accordingly, I find myself in a bind. Again, their unanimous judgment is that their near-death experiences were real beyond real. So, it is difficult for me to find a convincing reason to reject their judgment on that score while I would trust their medical judgments completely, even in life-or-death situations.

Now, as a professor of logic, I know full well that this is not a valid, rational argument in the technical sense. Rather, it is just that this kind of reasoning is all I have to go on when trying to come to terms with the challenging cognitive and spiritual conundrum of life after death.

This trust in the judgment of my colleagues explains in a large part why I, Raymond Moody, accept that there *is* a life beyond death.

What about other people, though? Is there some more general factor that applies to everyone?

That brings us to the third level of thinking about proof of life after death, namely, what is proof in the first place? And does it apply to the mysteries of conscious survival of physical death?

What Is Proof?

In my decades as a philosophy professor, researching and teaching on the question of postmortem consciousness survival, it always came back to the question: Do we have proof? Have we defined what *proof* is?

As discussed in the introduction, we know that proof is a rational means of leading everyone who follows it to the same logical conclusion, but there is so much more to this definition to consider, as we've discovered within these pages.

My philosophy courses concentrated on analyzing the most serious of obstacles to belief in the afterlife propounded by imminent thinkers. Historically, the real difficulties were pinpointed by two renowned British philosophers, David Hume (1711–1776) and A. J. Ayer (1910–1989). Hume correctly pointed out that proof of an afterlife would require logical principles beyond those which we have.[2] Ayer much later specified why logic as we know it fails. Namely, it is intelligible to say, for instance, that a person survived a complete change of personality, lifestyle, or belief. But it is completely unintelligible, Ayer went on, to declare that a person survived the annihilation of their individual body.[3]

What Hume and Ayer each pointed out are the actual real-life barriers that serious, rational proof of life after death must overcome. Logic as we know it operates with true-or-false statements of literal meaning. Claims about an afterlife, since they are unintelligible, are beyond that framework. Hence, ordinary logic is inadequate for proving an afterlife.

Hume and Ayer were right, and because they were right, their work pointed toward a solution of the difficulties they identified.

Ayer wrote about the unintelligibility of the notion of life after death in his classic book *Language, Truth and Logic*, in 1936. Ayer is one of my intellectual heroes, and I read his book in 1963 when I was an undergraduate philosophy major. Ayer's writing enabled many generations of philosophical readers to see for themselves that the notion of life after death has no determinable or intelligible meaning. His discussion was a wake-up call to anyone who entertained fantasies that proving life after death was a straightforward matter.

Then Ayer had a near-death experience in the late 1970s.

I heard directly from him what a big impact that had made on his life (transformation!) when we were both, a few years later, guests on a late-night BBC Radio program in London. Near-death experiences

(NDEs) was the topic of the discussion, and Ayer and I met in the green room before the broadcast. I felt truly humbled that he would discuss his near-death experience with me. I asked whether he thought his near-death experience might have been a delirium. And he responded immediately, emphatically, that it definitely was not. Ayer went further, telling me that he sensed that his experience was purposely meant and structured specifically for him. He felt some sentient presence, which he did not specify further, that was behind the individual planning of his experience.

Ayer's 1936 *The Unintelligibility of Talking about Life after Death*, was now to him—after having an NDE—unintelligible! He very much believed in life after life. Now he had to argue against his very own initial premise, and the line of inquiry he had closed was open again.

Nowadays, things are different. There is a growing realization that it is wise to put to rigorous study even unintelligible things that stymie the mind. New techniques have been devised, showing that even unintelligibility itself has a discernible structure with many different types and patterns and is no longer a practical obstacle to proof of life after death.

A new day is dawning in the serious study of life after death. That brings us to an eighth reason that supports there being an afterlife, and it brings the seven other reasons together, for the many human experiences we have surveyed can legitimately be thought of as proof of life after death. In other words, it is perfectly rational for us to anticipate, based on what we have learned, that our conscious selves will emerge in another framework of reality when we die. So, based upon the reality of a life beyond death, what should we do or think?

It really goes against my nature to offer personal advice. Besides, I am no shining exemplar of how people should go about managing their personal lives. Nonetheless, I am going to make an exception in this case because of the great suffering, great grief, and great tribulations so many of us are enduring.

You may be one of those who are mourning the loss of loved ones to death. You may be one of those who have been diagnosed with an incurable illness. You may be one of those who are growing older and beginning to wonder what life means in the final analysis. You may be one of those whose enjoyment of life is being severely restricted in persistent, intrusive fear of death. Or you may be one of those who are just naturally curious—irresistibly, intensely curious—about anything and everything.

If any of those descriptions fit you, then you might well be wondering and worrying about whether there really is life after death. And if so, I offer you some personal advice based on my sixty years of experience curiously studying this mystery: take heart. After decades of persistent, rigorous skeptical inquiry, I am confident of a life after death. So, I offer you these thoughts and this advice for what solace, comfort, consolation, or enlightenment they might bring you.

Yes, there really is a comforting, loving light at the end of the tunnel.

Acknowledgments

———————— ✳ ————————

Writing is a lonely profession. Yet ironically, it takes a village to complete a book, especially one with the daunting title of *Proof of Life after Life*.

To begin with, we would like to thank the dozens of people who shared their death experiences with us and with other researchers, some occurring centuries ago, all in the hopes of finding the *how*, *what*, and *why* of these paranormal experiences. Over the years we have communicated with thousands of people who have nearly died and have come back to tell of their amazing experience, or who have shared the death experiences of loved ones or even death experiences of people they do not know. It takes a significant amount of courage to tell these accounts, yet without them there would not be the field of death studies and no information with which to study the mysteries of death. At its essence, death studies is the study of stories. Without the proper record of these events, we would be lost. With them we find our way.

The study of consciousness—especially the survival of consciousness after death—is of endless interest to medical doctors, scientists, clergy people, and philosophers who are vexed by the age-old question, *what happens when we die?* It may seem absurd to go back thousands of years to thank Aristotle, Plato, and other great minds of ancient Greece who studied this question, but it is only fair that they be included in our acknowledgments. They formed the foundation for discussions of the possibility of an afterlife that we use even today. That goes for other early researchers such as Edmund Gurney, William Henry Frederic Myers, and Frank Podmore, who all devoted much of their lives to finding and examining the hundreds of case studies that make up their work, *Phantasms of the Living* (volumes I and II). These books set the bar for thoroughness and clear thinking in the world of death studies. The same can be said for the work of Sir William Barrett, a Dublin physicist whose book *Deathbed Visions* is a classic work in this field, one that led him to publicly state that its evidence proves a spiritual world and survival after death.

In modern times there are many researchers whose work is influential in death studies: Bruce Greyson, MD, whose overall studies created a path for other researchers to follow. Michael Nahm, PhD, who named and defined terminal lucidity and is pioneering death studies in many other ways. Jeffrey Long, MD, and his wife, Jody Long, founded the Near-Death Experience Research Foundation (NDERF) and are both among the finest thinkers in the field of death studies. The same is true of Dr. Ken Ring, whose pioneering work and spirit make him one of the leading foundational members of the near-death experience (NDE) movement. Melvin Morse, MD, has studied the transformative powers of the NDE in adults and children, leading to an understanding of the long-term effects of NDEs and other death experiences.

It was Michael Sabom, MD, who advanced the study of consciousness with his early studies of NDEs. He did not believe the "far-out" descriptions of NDEs presented in *Life After Life*, and he set out with Sarah Kreutziger, a psychiatric social worker, to uncover the truth. The result was *Recollections of Death*, a book that supported Raymond's work. Dr. Sabom, along with Dr. Moody, Dr. Greyson, John Audette, and Ken Ring, went on to found the International Association of Near-Death Studies.

Peter Fenwick, MD, a neuropsychiatrist and senior lecturer at King's College in London, England, is a fount of wisdom and research, especially as it pertains to shared death experiences (SDEs). So too is Penny Sartori, PhD, whose work as an intensive care nurse in England led to firsthand encounters with hundreds of NDE cases, some of which are detailed shared death experiences. Dutch cardiologist Pim van Lommel, MD, deserves accolades for his comprehensive study of 344 survivors of cardiac arrest and their near-death experiences, all of which has been compiled into his bestseller, *Consciousness beyond Life*, a massive study that has confirmed much of the existing NDE research.

The late George Ritchie, MD, was formidable in Raymond's life, a good friend and excellent teacher. He shared his NDE with Raymond and anyone who felt they needed to hear about it in all of its amazing aspects. The same is true of Eben Alexander, MD, who became a fast friend of Raymond's a few years before the publication of Eben's astounding bestseller, *Proof of Heaven*. He is a generous man who has shared his story with thousands of people and, along with his wife, Karen Newell, has broadened the world of holistic health with ongoing work in the field of sacred acoustics.

On the personal side, Raymond dedicates this book to his wife, Cheryl, whose strong personality, sense of humor, and perseverance are essential traits in a partner when living with a perpetual researcher. Raymond also dedicates this book to his four children: the older Avery, a medical doctor, and Samuel, a philosophy professor, both of whom are a source of great pride. Carter and Carol, Raymond's younger children, are a joy to observe as they make their way in life.

Paul dedicates this book to his wife, Darlene, who has always given the gift of support, understanding of the writing process, and encouragement. She is undoubtedly the highest bar in the family.

Paul and Raymond have worked together for nearly forty years, collaborated on six books, and made two movies. In the course of that time Paul has interviewed hundreds of people who have had NDEs, SDEs, and other types of death experiences. It's an honor to have worked so closely with Raymond, a teacher, muse, guide, and most importantly, a friend.

Finally, to the team at Beyond Words Publishing. Michele Ashtiani Cohn, creative director—who, along with her husband, Richard Cohn, publisher and president, saw something they liked in *Proof of Life after Life* and took it under their wings. Through them we were introduced to Bailey Potter, in whose hands the manuscript was expertly edited.

One can never underestimate the value of a good editor, especially when they can make a pair of writers better than they might be without her. Thanks to Lindsay Easterbooks-Brown, the managing editor, and her team: Emmalisa Sparrow Wood, production editor, Kristin Thiel, copy-editor, Ashley Van Winkle, proofreader, Brennah Hermo, marketing and publicity, Bill Brunson, typography, and Devon Smith, designer of the cover and the book's clean and readable interior. They are all, as their company name implies, beyond words.

Notes

Introduction: Beyond Near-Death Experiences

1. Raymond Moody, *Life After Life* (St. Simons Island, GA: Mockingbird Books, 1975).
2. William James, *The Varieties of Religious Experience* (Cambridge, MA: The Riverside Press, 1902), 226.
3. A version of "An SDE of My Own" was published in Raymond Moody, MD, with Paul Perry, *Glimpses of Eternity: Sharing a Loved One's Passage from This Life to the Next* (New York: Guideposts, 2010), 48–50.
4. C. S. Lewis, *Mere Christianity* (New York: Macmillan, 1952), 39.

Chapter 1: Shared Death Experiences

1. Gregory Vlastos, *Studies in Greek Philosophy*, vol. 2 (Princeton, NJ: Princeton University Press, 1995), 8.
2. Plato, "Phaedo," in *The Collected Dialogues of Plato*, eds. Edith Hamilton and Huntington Cairns (Princeton, NJ: Princeton University Press, 1961), 68.
3. Plato, *Phaedo*, trans. Edward Meredith Cope (Cambridge: The University Press, 1875), 20.
4. Plato, "Apology," in *The Dialogues of Plato*, trans. Benjamin Jowett (Oxford, UK: Oxford University Press, 1924), 133–34.
5. Louisa May Alcott, *Her Life, Letters, and Journals*, ed. Ednah Dow Littlehale Cheney (Boston: Little, Brown, and Company, 1919), 97–98.
6. Diane Goble, "Diane G NDE," Near Death Experience Research Foundation, accessed January 4, 2023, https://www.nderf.org/Experiences/1diane_g_nde.html.
7. Raymond Moody interview with an SDEr, 2019.

8. Erlendur Haraldsson (Icelandic psychologist and author of *I Saw a Light and Came Here*) in personal communication with Paul Perry, March 1990, 1995, 2000.

9. Melvin Morse and Paul Perry, *Transformed by the Light: The Powerful Effect of Near-Death Experiences on People's Lives* (New York: Villard Books, 1992), 58–60.

10. Melvin Morse (afterlife researcher and author of *Closer to the Light* with Paul Perry), in discussion with Raymond Moody and Paul Perry at a conference in Seattle, Washington, 1989.

11. C. G. Jung, *Jung on Death and Immortality*, ed. Jenny Yates (Princeton, NJ: Princeton University Press, 1999), 156.

12. Alexander Batthyany, PhD (director of the Viktor Frankl Institute), in discussion with Paul Perry, 2020.

13. D. Scott Rogo, *A Psychic Study of "the Music of the Spheres"* (Ann Arbor, MI: University of Michigan, 1972), 64–66.

14. Michael Nahm, "Terminal Lucidity in People with Mental Illness and Other Mental Disability: An Overview and Implications for Possible Explanatory Models," *Journal of Near-Death Studies* 28, no. 2 (Winter 2009): 90, accessed February 7, 2023, https://digital.library.unt.edu/ark:/67531/metadc461761/.

15. Raymond Moody interview with a psychomanteum client, 1991.

16. Joan Rivers (comedian, actress, and producer) in discussion with Raymond Moody, 1992.

17. *The Oprah Winfrey Show*, season 8, episode 208, "Communicating with the Dead," aired October 18, 1993, syndicated.

Chapter 2: Reason #1: Out-of-Body Experiences

1. Queen Noor, *Leap of Faith: Memoirs of an Unexpected Life* (New York: Miramax Books, 2003), 236.

2. Noor, *Leap of Faith*, 236.

3. An NDEr, in discussion with Paul Perry at a conference in Santa Barbara, California, 2018.

4. Raymond Moody interview with a surgeon at a conference in Milan, Italy, 2010.

5. Melvin Morse (afterlife researcher and author of *Closer to the Light* with Paul Perry), in discussion with Raymond Moody and Paul Perry, circa 1993.

6. Raymond Moody interview with Viola Horton, her family, and attending physician, 1975; Case study was included in Peter Shockey (director), *Life After Life*, documentary starring Raymond Moody, 1992; Viola Horton's account presented by Raymond Moody and The Learning Channel at "Near Death Experience with Many Verified Events Proving It Was Real, Dr. Morse Presents," Melvin Morse, February 28, 2011, https://www.you tube.com/watch?v=MFCnPOTCYJE.

7. A version of this story was published in Raymond Moody, MD, with Paul Perry, *Glimpses of Eternity: Sharing a Loved One's Passage from This Life to the Next* (New York: Guideposts, 2010), 90–91.

8. Raymond Moody interview with physician, circa 1989.

9. Events from Raymond Moody's discussions and correspondence with Michael Sabom and Sarah Kreutziger, circa 1977.

10. Michael B. Sabom, *Recollections of Death: A Medical Investigation* (New York: HarperCollins, 1982).

11. Sabom, *Recollections of Death*, 36.

12. Sabom, *Recollections of Death*, 106.

13. Sabom, *Recollections of Death*, 30–31.

14. Sabom, *Recollections of Death*, 26.

15. Sabom, *Recollections of Death*, 36.

16. Sabom, *Recollections of Death*, 84.

17. Penny Sartori, "A Long-Term Study to Investigate the Incidence and Phenomenology of Near-Death Experiences in a Welsh Intensive Therapy Unit," *Network Review: Journal of the Scientific and Medical Network*, no. 90 (Spring 2006), republished on the International Association for Near-Death Studies website, https://iands.org/research/nde-research /important-research-articles/80-penny-sartori-phd-prospective-study .html?start=1.

18. Sartori, "Long-Term Study."

19. Janice M. Holden, "More Things in Heaven and Earth: A Response to 'Near-Death Experiences with Hallucinatory Features,'" *Journal of Near-Death Studies* 26, no. 1 (Fall 2007): 40, https://digital.library.unt.edu /ark:/67531/metadc799193/m2/1/high_res_d/vol26-no1-33.pdf.

20. Holden, "More Things," 40.

21. Holden, "More Things," 40.

22. Holden, "More Things," 40.

23. Jeffrey Long, "Near-Death Experiences Evidence for Their Reality," *Journal of the Missouri State Medical Association* 111, no. 5 (September–

October 2014): 372–80, https://www.ncbi.nlm.nih.gov/pmc/articles/PMC6172100/.

24. Long, "Near-Death Experiences," 374.

25. Long, "Near-Death Experiences," 374.

26. Long, "Near-Death Experiences," 374.

27. Long, "Near-Death Experiences," 374.

28. Long, "Near-Death Experiences," 374.

29. Jeffrey Long, "Evidence for Survival of Consciousness in Near-Death Experiences: Decades of Science and New Insights," July 21, 2021, https://theformulaforcreatingheavenonearth.com/wp-content/uploads/2022/04/05-RU-Jeffrey-Long.pdf.

30. Long, "Evidence for Survival of Consciousness," 10–11; Kate L NDE, Near Death Experience Research Foundation, https://www.nderf.org/Experiences/1kate_l_nde.html.

31. Long, "Evidence for Survival of Consciousness," 11.

32. Paul Perry interview with Jeffrey Long, circa 2010–2012.

33. Perry interview with Jeffrey Long.

34. Perry interview with Jeffrey Long.

35. Jeffrey Long with Paul Perry, God and the Afterlife: The Groundbreaking New Evidence for God and Near-Death Experience (New York: HarperOne, 2016).

36. Perry interview with Jeffrey Long.

37. Perry interview with Jeffrey Long.

38. Long, "Evidence for Survival of Consciousness," 11.

39. Long, "Evidence for Survival of Consciousness," 11.

40. Long, "Evidence for Survival of Consciousness," 12.

41. Long, "Evidence for Survival of Consciousness," 12.

42. Perry interview with Jeffrey Long.

43. Perry interview with Jeffrey Long.

44. Charlotte Marial et al., "Temporality of Features in Near-Death Experience Narratives," Frontiers in Human Neuroscience 11 (2017): table 4, https://www.frontiersin.org/articles/10.3389/fnhum.2017.00311/full.

45. "Key Facts about Near-Death Experiences," International Association for Near-Death Studies website, last updated July 18, 2021, https://iands.org/ndes/about-ndes/key-nde-facts21.html?start=1.

46. George Ritchie (American psychiatrist and author of Ordered to Return: My Life After Dying), in discussions with Raymond Moody over the course of their nearly thirty-year friendship.

47. George Ritchie, discussions.
48. "Wilder Penfield (1891–1976)," McGill University website, accessed February 8, 2023, https://www.mcgill.ca/about/history/penfield.
49. Laura Mazzola, Jean Isnard, Roland Peyron, and Francois Mauguiere, "Stimulation of the Human Cortex and the Experience of Pain: Wilder Penfield's Observations Revisited," *Brain* 135, no. 2 (February 2012): 631–40, https://doi.org/10.1093/brain/awr265.
50. Richard Leblanc, "The White Paper: Wilder Penfield, Stream of Consciousness, and the Physiology of Mind," *Journal of the History of the Neurosciences* 28, no. 4 (2019): 416–36, https://doi.org/10.1080/0964704X.2019.1651135.
51. Wilder Penfield, *The Mystery of the Mind* (Princeton, NJ: Princeton University Press, 1975), 85–87.
52. Penfield, *The Mystery of the Mind*, 115.

Chapter 3: Reason #2: Precognitive Experiences

1. Sir William Barrett, *Death-Bed Visions: The Psychical Experiences of the Dying* (Detroit: Aquarian Press, 1986), 162.
2. Raymond Moody in interview with an SDEr, January 7, 2023.
3. Edmund Gurney, Frederic Myers, and Frank Podmore, *Phantasms of the Living*, vol. 2 (London: Rooms of the Society for Psychical Research, 1886), 182; a version of this story was published in Moody with Perry, *Glimpses of Eternity*, 109–110.
4. Gurney, Myers, and Podmore, *Phantasms of the Living*.
5. Gurney, Myers, and Podmore, *Phantasms of the Living*.
6. Gurney, Myers, and Podmore, *Phantasms of the Living*.
7. Sir William Barrett, *Death-Bed Visions: How the Dead Talk to the Dying* (United Kingdom: White Crow Books, 2011), 59.
8. Raymond Moody in interview with an SDEr, 2009; a version of this story was published in Moody with Perry, *Glimpses of Eternity*, 144.
9. Moody in interview with an SDEr, 2005.
10. Gurney, Myers, and Podmore, *Phantasms*, vol. 2, 235.
11. Perry interview with an SDEr, January 15, 2023.
12. A version of this story was published in Moody with Perry, *Glimpses of Eternity*, 59–62; a version of this story was also published in Melvin Morse, MD, and Paul Perry, *Parting Visions* (New York: HarperPaperbacks), 19–21.

13. Morse and Perry, *Parting Visions*, 45.
14. Morse and Perry, *Parting Visions*, 45.
15. Morse and Perry, *Parting Visions*, 46–48.
16. University of Missouri-Columbia, "People Who Rely on Their Intuition Are, at Times, Less Likely to Cheat," *ScienceDaily*, November 24, 2015, https://www.sciencedaily.com/releases/2015/11/151124143502.htm.
17. C. G. Jung, *Jung on Synchronicity and the Paranormal* (Princeton, NJ: Princeton University Press, 1997), 58-59.
18. Erlendur Haraldsson et al., "Psychic Experiences in the Multinational Human Value Study: Who Reports Them?," *Journal of the American Society for Psychical Research* 85 (April 1991): 150.
19. Erlendur Haraldsson, "Survey of Claimed Encounters with the Dead," *Omega* 19, no. 2 (1988–1989): 105, efaidnbmnnnibpcajpcglclefindmkaj/https://notendur.hi.is/erlendur/english/Apparitions/omega.pdf.
20. Haraldsson, "Survey of Claimed Encounters with the Dead," table 3, 110.
21. Haraldsson, "Survey of Claimed Encounters with the Dead," 106.
22. Haraldsson, "Survey of Claimed Encounters with the Dead," table 1, 106–107.
23. Haraldsson, "Survey of Claimed Encounters with the Dead," table 2, 109.
24. Erlendur Haraldsson (professor of psychology at the University of Iceland), in discussion and correspondence with Paul Perry, circa 1988.
25. Haraldsson, "Survey of Claimed Encounters with the Dead," 104.
26. Haraldsson, "Survey of Claimed Encounters with the Dead," table 2, 109–110.
27. Haraldsson, in discussion and correspondence with Perry, circa 1988.
28. Haraldsson, in discussion and correspondence with Perry, circa 1988.
29. Haraldsson, "Survey of Claimed Encounters with the Dead," 111.
30. Erlendur Haraldsson, in discussion and correspondence with Perry, circa 1988.
31. Erlendur Haraldsson, in discussion and correspondence with Perry, circa 1988.
32. Erlendur Haraldsson, in discussion and correspondence with Perry, circa 1988.
33. Stephen Hawking, *A Brief History of Time* (New York: Bantom, 1998), 1.

Chapter 4: Reason #3: The Transforming Light

1. Charles Dickens, *A Christmas Carol* (Orinda, CA: SeaWolf Press, 2019), 17–18.
2. Dickens, *A Christmas Carol*, 2.
3. Charles Flynn, "Meanings and Implications of NDEr Transformations: Some Preliminary Findings and Implications," *Journal of Near-Death Studies* 2, no. 1 (June 1982): 3, https://digital.library.unt.edu/ark:/67531/metadc1051956/.
4. Melvin Morse and Paul Perry, *Transformed by the Light: The Powerful Effect of Near-Death Experiences on People's Lives* (New York: Villard Books, 1992), 29.
5. Morse and Perry, *Transformed by the Light*, 58–60.
6. Raymond Moody in interview with an SDEr, circa 1992.
7. Moody in interview with an SDEr, circa 1991.
8. Moody in interview with an NDEr, 2021.
9. Moody in interview with an NDEr, 1991.
10. Moody in interview with an NDEr, 2010.
11. Moody in interview with an NDEr, 1991.
12. Moody in interview with an NDEr, 2009.
13. Michael Eden, "Brain Surgery Left Me with Special Gift, Says Herefordshire Modeller," *Hereford Times*, October 22, 2022, https://www.herefordtimes.com/news/23068056.brain-injury-made-ace-modeller-says-herefordshire-man/.
14. Moody in interview with an NDEr, 2010.
15. Moody in interview with an NDEr, circa 1991.
16. Plato, *The Republic*, trans. Desmond Lee (London: Penguin Classics, 2007).
17. Moody in interview with an NDEr, circa 1992.
18. Guidelines for "How to Support an NDEr" gathered during an afterlife conference in Seattle led by Raymond Moody with a panel of researchers including Melvin Morse and Paul Perry, circa 1990.
19. A version of this story was published in Morse and Perry, *Transformed by the Light*, 74.
20. Melvin Morse and Paul Perry, *Closer to the Light: Learning from the Near-Death Experiences of Children* (New York City, NY: Villard Books 1990), 152.

21. Morse and Perry, *Closer to the Light*, 151-53.
22. Morse and Perry, *Closer to the Light*, 153.
23. Dickens, *A Christmas Carol*, 94.
24. Plato, *The Republic*, 329a–331c.

Chapter 5: Reason #4: Terminal Lucidity

1. Michael Nahm and Bruce Greyson, "The Death of Anna Katharina Ehmer: A Case Study in Terminal Lucidity," *Omega* 68, no. 1 (2013–2014): 81–82, https://www.researchgate.net/publication/260250637_The_Death_of_Anna_Katharina_Ehmer_A_Case_Study_in_Terminal_Lucidity.
2. Nahm and Greyson, "The Death of Anna Katharina Ehmer," 82.
3. Nahm and Greyson, "The Death of Anna Katharina Ehmer," 82–83.
4. Nahm and Greyson, "The Death of Anna Katharina Ehmer," 83.
5. Nahm and Greyson, "The Death of Anna Katharina Ehmer," 84.
6. Nahm and Greyson, "The Death of Anna Katharina Ehmer," 82.
7. Nahm and Greyson, "The Death of Anna Katharina Ehmer," 83.
8. A. D. (Sandy) Macleod, "Lightening Up Before Death," *Palliative & Supportive Care* 7, no. 4 (2009): 513–516, https://doi.org/10.1017/S1478951509990526.
9. Alexander Batthyány, PhD (director of the Research Institute for Theoretical Psychology and Personalist Studies at Pázmány University, Budapest), in discussion with Paul Perry, 2021.
10. Michael Nahm (afterlife researcher, biologist, and parapsychologist), in discussion with Paul Perry, 2021.
11. Michael Nahm, "Terminal Lucidity in People with Mental Illness and Other Mental Disability: An Overview and Implications for Possible Explanatory Models," *Journal of Near-Death Studies* 28, no. 2 (Winter 2009): 89, accessed February 7, 2023, https://digital.library.unt.edu/ark:/67531/metadc461761/.
12. Nahm, in discussion with Paul Perry, 2021; Michael Nahm, "Terminal Lucidity Versus Paradoxical Lucidity: A Terminological Clarification," *Alzheimer's & Dementia* 18, no. 3 (March 2022): 538–39, https://doi.org/10.1002/alz.12574.
13. Nahm, "Terminal Lucidity in People with Mental Illness."
14. Basil Eldadah, "Exploring the Unexpected: What Can We Learn from Lucidity in Dementia?," National Institute on Aging, September 11, 2019, https://

www.nia.nih.gov/research/blog/2019/09/exploring-unexpected-what-can
-we-learn-lucidity-dementia.

15. René Descartes, *Discourse on Method and Meditations*, trans. Elizabeth Sanderson Haldane, G. R. T. Ross (New York: Dover Publications, 2003), 23.

16. Scott Haig, MD, "The Brain: The Power of Hope," *Time*, January 29, 2007, http://content.time.com/time/magazine/article/0,9171,1580392-1,00 .html.

17. Jewel Perry (Paul Perry's father and WWII veteran), in discussion with Paul Perry, 1995.

18. Nahm in discussion with Perry, 2020.

19. James Fieser, "Continental Rationalism," University of Tennessee at Martin, revised June 1, 2020, https://www.utm.edu/staff/jfieser/class/110/7 -rationalism.htm, from Samuel Enoch Stumpf and James Fieser, *Philosophy: A Historical Survey with Essential Readings*, 10th ed. (New York: McGraw Hill, 2019).

20. Michael Nahm, interview by Zaron Burnett III, "Terminal Lucidity: The Researchers Attempting to Prove Your Mind Lives on Even after You Die," *Mel Magazine*, September 26, 2018, https://medium.com/mel-magazine /terminal-lucidity-the-researchers-attempting-to-prove-that-your-mind -lives-on-even-after-you-die-385ac1f93dca.

21. Basil A. Eldadah, et al., "Lucidity in Dementia: A Perspective from the NIA," *Alzheimer's & Dementia* 15 (2019): 1104–1106, https://www.science direct.com/science/article/pii/S1552526019340804.

22. Nahm, "Terminal Lucidity in People with Mental Illness," 91.

23. Nahm, "Terminal Lucidity in People with Mental Illness," 90.

24. Nahm, "Terminal Lucidity in People with Mental Illness," 91.

25. Alexandre Jacques François Brierre de Boismont, *Hallucinations, or, The Rational History of Apparitions, Visions, Dreams, Ecstasy, Magnetism, and Somnambulism* (Philadelphia: Lindsay and Blakiston, 1853), 243.

26. Benjamin Rush, *Medial Inquiries and Observations, Upon the Diseases of the Mind* (Philadelphia: Kimber & Richardson, 1812), 257.

27. Andrew Marshal and Solomon Sawrey, *The Morbid Anatomy of the Brain in Mania and Hydrophobia: With the Pathology of These Two Diseases as Collected from the Papers of the Late Andrew Marshal* (London: Longman, Hurst, Rees, Orme & Brown, 1815), 150–51.

28. Aristotle, *De Anima*, trans. R. D. Hicks (New York: Cosimo Classics, 2008) 73.

29. Libre Texts, "Chapter 12: Peripheral Nervous System—12.1A: Over-view of Sensation," in *Anatomy and Physiology (Boundless)*, 362-63, updated January 17, 2023, https://med.libretexts.org/Bookshelve/Anatomys_and_Physiology/Anatomy_and_Physiology_(Boundless)/12%3A_Peripheral_Nervous_System/12.1%3A_Sensation/12.1A%3A_Overview_of_Sensation.pdf.

30. Wilder Penfield, *The Mystery of the Mind* (Princeton, NJ: Princeton University Press, 1975), 88.

31. Paul Perry in interview with an SDEr, November 2022.

32. Raymond Moody interview with an SDEr, Afterlife Awareness Conference, Portland, OR, June 2014.

33. Peter Fenwick and Elizabeth Fenwick, *The Art of Dying: A Journey to Elsewhere* (London: Continuum, 2008), 91.

34. Peter Fenwick, "Dying: A Spiritual Experience as Shown by Near Death Experiences and Deathbed Visions," Royal College of Psychiatrists publications archive, https://www.rcpsych.ac.uk/docs/default-source/members/sigs/spirituality-spsig/spirituality-special-interest-group-publications-pfenwickneardeath.pdf.

35. "Julie P.'s NELE," After Death Communication Research Foundation (ADCRF), accessed February 8, 2023, https://www.adcrf.org/julie_p_nele.htm.

36. "Julie P.'s NELE," After Death Communication Research Foundation.

37. "Julie P.'s NELE," After Death Communication Research Foundation.

38. J. C Eccles, *Facing Reality: Philosophical Adventures by a Brain Scientist* (New York: Springer-Verlag, 1970), 56.

39. Judith Matloff, "The Mystery of End-of-Life Rallies," *New York Times*, July 24, 2018, https://www.nytimes.com/2018/07/24/well/the-mystery-of-end-of-life-rallies.html.

40. Natasha A. Tassell-Matamua, PhD, and Kate Steadman, "Of Love and Light: A Case Report of End-of-Life Experiences," *Journal of Near-Death Studies* 34, no. 1 (Fall 2015), 12, https://doi.org/10.17514/jnds-2015-34-1-p5-26.

41. Tassell-Matamua and Steadman, "Of Love and Light," 13.

42. Tassell-Matamua and Steadman, "Of Love and Light," 15–16.

43. Karlis Osis and Erlendur Haraldsson, *At the Hour of Death* (New York: Hastings House, 1995).

44. Osis and Haraldsson, *At the Hour of Death*, 40.

45. John H. Lienhard, *Engines of Our Ingenuity*, episode 2077, "Last Words," University of Houston's College of Engineering, transcript and audio, KUHO, Houston Public Radio, n.d., mp3, https://www.uh.edu/engines /epi2077.htm.

46. Francis Crick, *The Astonishing Hypothesis: The Scientific Search for the Soul* (New York: Touchstone, Simon and Schuster, July 1995), 3.

Chapter 6: Reason #5: Spontaneous Muses, Healings, and Skills

1. Lawrence G. Appelbaum et al., "Synaptic Plasticity and Mental Health: Methods, Challengese and Opportunities," *Neuropsychopharmacology* 48, no. 1 (January 2023): 113–120, https://www.ncbi.nlm.nih.gov/pmc/articles /PMC9700665/.

2. Frederick Ayer, Jr., *Before the Colors Fade: A Portrait of a Soldier: George S. Patton, Jr* (New York: Houghton Mifflin, 1964), 98.

3. Ayer, Jr., *Before the Colors Fade*, 97–98.

4. Rajiv Parti, MD (consciousness-based healer, pain management specialist, heart anesthesiologist), in discussion with Raymond Moody, January 9, 2014.

5. Dr. Rajiv Parti and Paul Perry, *Dying to Wake Up* (New York: Atria, 2017), 30.

6. Parti, *Dying to Wake Up*, 55.

7. Parti, *Dying to Wake Up*, xiii.

8. Parti, *Dying to Wake Up*, xiv.

9. Parti, *Dying to Wake Up*, 58.

10. Parti, *Dying to Wake Up*, 63.

11. Parti, *Dying to Wake Up*, 163-64.

12. Frank Herbert, *Dune* (New York: Berkley Medallion Books, 1977), 31.

13. "Sanna F SDE," Near-Death Experience Research Foundation website, 5117 Sanna F SDE 9509, accessed February 9, 2023, https://www.nderf .org/Experiences/1sanna_f_sde.html.

14. "Sanna F SDE," https://www.nderf.org/Experiences/1sanna_f_sde.html.

15. "Sanna F SDE," https://www.nderf.org/Experiences/1sanna_f_sde.html.

16. Sanna Festa, email to Paul Perry, January 5, 2023.

17. Sanna Festa, email to Perry.

18. Sanna Festa, email to Perry.

19. Penny Sartori, Paul Badham, and Peter Fenwick, "A Prospectively Studied Near-Death Experience with Corroborated Out-of-Body Perceptions and Unexplained Healing," *Journal of Near-Death Science* 25, no. 2 (Winter 2006): 73, https://digital.library.unt.edu/ark:/67531/metadc799351/m2/1/high_res_d/vol25-no2-69.pdf

20. Sartori, Badham, and Fenwick, "A Prospectively Studied," 73.

21. Sartori, Badham, and Fenwick, "A Prospectively Studied," 73.

22. Sartori, Badham, and Fenwick, "A Prospectively Studied," 69–82.

23. Penny Sartori, "Ex-Nurse Dr. Penny Sartori Studies Amazing Experiences of People Who Came Back from the Dead," interviewed by Brian McIver, *The Daily Record*, January 25, 2011, https://www.dailyrecord.co.uk/news/real-life/ex-nurse-dr-penny-sartori-studies-1093165.

24. Paul Perry in interview with an SDEr, January 21, 2023.

25. Tony Cicoria, MD (orthopedic surgeon), quote from discussion and correspondence with Raymond Moody and Paul Perry, circa 2018; Tony Cicoria and Jordan Cicoria, "Getting Comfortable with Near-Death Experiences—My Near-Death Experience: a Telephone Call from God," *Journal of the Missouri State Medical Association* 111, n. 4 (2014): 304, https://www.ncbi.nlm.nih.gov/pmc/articles/PMC6179462/.

26. Cicoria, "My Near-Death Experience," 304.

27. Cicoria, "My Near-Death Experience," 305.

28. Cicoria, "My Near-Death Experience," 305.

29. Cicoria, discussion and correspondence with Moody and Perry.

30. Cicoria, "My Near-Death Experience," 305.

31. Cicoria, "My Near-Death Experience," 305.

32. Tony Cicoria, MD, "The Electrifying Story of The Accidental Pianist & Composer," *Missouri Medicine* 111, no. 4 (Jul–Aug 2014): 308, https://www.ncbi.nlm.nih.gov/pmc/articles/PMC6179476/.

33. Cicoria, "The Electrifying Story of The Accidental Pianist," 308.

34. "NY Surgeon Survives Lightning Strike and Discovers a Surprising Musical Ability," *Orthopedics Today*, August 1, 2009.

35. Cicoria, "The Electrifying Story of The Accidental Pianist," 308.

36. "NY Surgeon Survives Lightning Strike," *Orthopedics Today*.

37. Oliver Sacks, *Musicophilia* (New York, NY: Alfred A. Knopf, 2008), 7.

38. Cicoria, "My Near-Death Experience," 307.

39. Cicoria, "My Near-Death Experience," 307.

Chapter 7: Reason #6: Light, Mist, and Music

1. A version of this story was published in Raymond Moody, MD, with Paul Perry, *Glimpses of Eternity: Sharing a Loved One's Passage from This Life to the Next* (New York: Guideposts, 2010), 5–8.
2. Carl Gustav Jung, *Memories, Dreams, Reflections* (New York: Vintage Books, 1989), 289.
3. Raymond Moody in interview with an SDEr (home care hospice nurse), circa 2010.
4. Hans Martensen-Larsen, *Ein Schimmer Durch den Vorhang* (Berlin: Furche Verlag, 1930), 26, translated by Michael Nahm (published in his German book *Wenn die Dunkelheit ein Ende findet-Terminale Geistesklarheit und andere Phänomene in Todesnähe* (Amerang: Crotona Verlag, 2020) and shared with Paul Perry in correspondence, circa 2020.
5. A version of this story was published in Raymond Moody, MD, with Paul Perry, *Glimpses of Eternity: Sharing a Loved One's Passage from This Life to the Next* (New York: Guideposts, 2010), 85.
6. Raymond Moody in interview with an SDEr, circa 2009.
7. Melvin Morse and Paul Perry, *Transformed by the Light: The Powerful Effect of Near-Death Experiences on People's Lives* (New York: Villard Books, 1992), 58.
8. Morse and Perry, *Transformed by the Light*, 58.
9. Paul Perry in interview with an SDEr, 2019.
10. Catherine Johnston and Rebecca Nappi, "EndNotes: A Nurse's Tale: The Spirit Leaves the Body," *Spokesman-Review*, July 12, 2012, https://www.spokesman.com/blogs/endnotes/2012/jul/12/nurses-tale-spirit-leaves-body/.
11. Peter Fenwick and Elizabeth Fenwick, *The Art of Dying* (New York: Bloomsbury Academic, 2008), 160–61.
12. Robert Crookall, *Out of the Body Experiences* (New York: Citadel Press Books, 1992), 153, https://archive.org/details/robertcrookalloutofthebodyexperiences/page/n5/mode/2up.
13. Raymond Moody in interview with an SDEr, circa 1999.
14. Raymond Moody in interview with an SDEr, 2010.
15. Otto Meinardus, PhD (theologian), in discussion with Paul Perry, 2005.
16. John W. Edmonds, *Spiritualism*, ed. George T. Dexter (New York: Cambridge University Press, 2011), 166.

17. Jeff Olsen and Jeff O'Driscoll, "Their Shared Near-Death Experience Formed an Unbreakable Bond," *Guideposts*, accessed February 8, 2023, https://guideposts.org/angels-and-miracles/life-after-death/their-shared-near-death-experience-formed-an-unbreakable-bond/; and in interview with Perry in 1999.
18. Olsen and O'Driscoll, *Guideposts*.
19. Olsen and O'Driscoll, *Guideposts*.
20. Moody and Perry in interview with two SDErs (Jeff Olsen and Jeff O'Driscoll), 2010-present day; "The Near-Death Experience of Jeff Olsen," YouTube, interview with Anthony Chene, Anthony Chene Production, 46:55, https://www.youtube.com/watch?v=1FD5lReqe64; Jeff O'Driscoll, https://www.jeffodriscoll.com.
21. Raymond Moody interview with a psychologist.
22. Paul Perry interview with an SDEr, circa 2015.
23. George Ritchie (American psychiatrist and author of *Ordered to Return: My Life After Dying*), in discussions with Raymond Moody over the course of their nearly thirty-year friendship.
24. Moody Interview with an SDEr, circa 2015.
25. Barrett, *Death-Bed Visions*, 97, originally from Gurney, Myers, and Podmore, *Phantasms of the Living*, vol. 2, 639.
26. Gurney, Myers, Podmore, *Phantasms of the Living*, 98, originally from Edmund Gurney, Frederic Myers, and Frank Podmore, *Phantasms of the Living*, vol. 2 (London: Rooms of the Society for Psychical Research, 1886), 639.
27. Gurney, Myers, Podmore, *Phantasms of the Living*, 98, originally from Gurney, Myers, and Podmore, *Phantasms of the Living*, vol. 2, 641.
28. A version of this story was published in Raymond Moody, MD, with Paul Perry, *Glimpses of Eternity: Sharing a Loved One's Passage from This Life to the Next* (New York: Guideposts, 2010), 145.
29. Gurney, Myers, and Podmore, *Phantasms of the Living*, vol. 2, 223.
30. Gurney, Myers, and Podmore, *Phantasms of the Living*, vol. 2, 203.
31. Gurney, Myers, and Podmore, *Phantasms of the Living*, vol. 2, 202–3.
32. Gurney, Myers, and Podmore, *Phantasms of the Living*, vol. 2, 203.
33. Moody in interview with an SDEr, circa 2009.
34. Peter Fenwick, Hilary Lovelace, and Sue Brayne, "Comfort for the Dying: Five Year Retrospective and One Year Prospective Studies of End of Life Experiences," *Archives of Gerontology and Geriatrics* 51, no. 2 (September–October 2010): 4 https://www.academia.edu/22946305/Comfort_for_the

_dying_five_year_retrospective_and_one_year_prospective_studies_of_
end_of_life_experiences.

35. Fenwick "Comfort for the Dying," 4.

Chapter 8: Reason #7: The Psychomanteum

1. Raymond A. Moody, Jr, PhD, MD, "Family Reunions: Visionary Encounters with the Departed in a Modern-Day Psychomanteum," *Journal of Near-Death Studies* 11, no. 2 (December 1992): 83–121, https://digital .library.unt.edu/ark:/67531/metadc799174/m2/1/high_res_d/vol11 -no2-83.pdf.

2. Arthur Hastings, PhD, "Effects on Bereavement Using a Restricted Sensory Environment Psychomanteum," *The Journal of Transpersonal Psychology* 44, no. 1 (2012): 4, https://atpweb.org/jtparchive/trps-44-12 -01-000.pdf.

3. Hastings, "Effects on Bereavement," 7.

4. Hastings, "Effects on Bereavement," 11.

5. Hastings, "Effects on Bereavement," 7.

6. Raymond Moody interview with a psychomanteum patient, 1990.

7. Sotiris Dakaris (classical Greek archeologist), in discussion with Raymond Moody, 1989–1991.

8. Homer, *The Odyssey*, trans. W. H. D. Rouse (New York: Penguin Publishing Group, 2015), 11.38–40.

9. *The Odyssey*, 11.43.

10. *The Odyssey*, 11.204–206.

11. Erlendur Haraldsson, "Survey of Claimed Encounters with the Dead," *OMEGA - Journal of Death and Dying* 19, no. 2 (October 1989): 105, https://doi.org/10.2190/nuyd-ax5d-lp2c-nux5.

12. Salvador Dalí, 50 *Secrets of Magical Craftsmanship* (New York: Dover Publications, 1992), 33–38.

13. Bret Stetka, "Spark Creativity with Thomas Edison's Napping Technique," *Scientific American*, December 9, 2021, https://www.scientificamerican.com /article/thomas-edisons-naps-inspire-a-way-to-spark-your-own-creativity/.

14. Moody in interview with psychomanteum patient, circa 1990.

15. Moody in interview with psychomanteum patient, circa 1991.

16. Moody in interview with psychomanteum patient, circa 1990.

17. Moody in interview with psychomanteum patient, circa 1994.

18. Moody in interview with psychomanteum patient, circa 1992.

19. Moody, "Family Reunions," 110.
20. Moody, "Family Reunions," 110.
21. A version of this story was published in Moody, "Family Reunions," 111–113.
22. Raymond Moody and Paul Perry, *Reunions* (New York: Random House Publishing, 1994), 96.
23. Raymond Moody and Paul Perry in interview with psychomanteum patient, circa 1991; Moody, Perry, *Reunions*, 96–97; a version of this story was published in Moody, "Family Reunions," 110–112.
24. Raymond Moody interview with a psychomanteum patient, circa 1991.
25. Raymond Mood interview with a psychomanteum patient, circa 1990.
26. Raymond Moody , "Family Reunions," 111.
27. *The Oprah Winfrey Show*, season 8, episode 208, "Communicating with the Dead," aired October 18, 1993, syndicated.
28. Joan Rivers (comedian, actress, and producer), in discussion with Raymond Moody, 1992.
29. Moody, Perry, *Reunions*, 90.
30. Moody, Perry, *Reunions*, 90.
31. Moody, Perry, *Reunions*, 95.
32. Moody, Perry, *Reunions*, 96.
33. Moody, Perry, *Reunions*, 97.
34. Moody, Perry, *Reunions*, 98.
35. Moody interview with a psychomanteum patient, 2011; Paul Perry (dir.), *The Light Beyond: A Talkumentary with Raymond Moody, MD, on Life, Death and the Pursuit of the Afterlife*, starring Raymond Moody, Beyond Words Publishing, December 6, 2016, DVD and VOD, 1 hour 20 minutes, story told 1:08–1:10.
36. Black Swan, "About," Hasso Plattner Institut, accessed December 29, 2022, http://blackswanevents.org/?page_id=26.
37. Nassim Nicholas Taleb, *Fooled by Randomness: The Hidden Role of Chance in Life and in the Markets*, 2nd ed. (New York: Random House, 2005), 117.

Conclusion

1. Plato, "Phaedo," in *The Collected Dialogues of Plato*, eds. Edith Hamilton and Huntington Cairns (Princeton, NJ: Princeton University Press, 1961), 95.

2. David Hume, *Dialogues and Natural History of Religion* (New York: Oxford University Press, 2009).

3. A. J. Ayer, "What I Saw When I was Dead," *The Sunday Telegraph*, August 28, 1988, reprinted in Dr. Peter Sjöstedt-Hughes, "Philosopher of Mind and Metaphysics," accessed December 22, 2022, http://www.philosopher .eu/others-writings/a-j-ayer-what-i-saw-when-i-was-dead/.

Discussion Questions:

1. Felix Salten, *Bambi* (Los Angeles: RKO Radio Pictures, 1942), filmscript on Scritps.com, accessed March 23, 2023, https://www.scripts.com/script /bambi_3526#google_vignette.

2. W. K. C. Guthrie, *A History of Greek Philosophy: Volume One: The Earlier Presocratic and the Pythagoreans, Revised Edition* (Cambridge, UK: Cambridge University Press, 1979).

3. Pim van Lommel, MD, *The Science of the Near-Death Experience* (Columbia: University of Missouri Press, 2017), 45–47.

Frequently Asked Questions

───────────✳───────────

1. Can one prepare for a positive life review?

Life reviews are among the most thought-provoking aspects of the near-death experience (NDE). The thought of reviewing one's life in detail is difficult for some to swallow. After all, NDErs not only review their own lives but the lives of the people they have interacted with, namely, sensing how they made the other person feel. This can be negative and painful if they were unkind to the other person, or very positive if they were gracious and kind. In the case of a shared death experience, the thoughts of a loved one reviewing their life in intimate detail are doubly difficult to imagine.

This has led some people to turn the life review into a regular spiritual practice now. They strive constantly to keep in mind that they will see again everything they do, from all perspectives. They think before reacting, making certain to respond to someone else's anger with kindness, choosing to act justly even when no one else notices, and following the advice Thumper's mother makes him recite after he speaks unkind words about Bambi, namely, "If you can't say something nice, don't say nothing at all."[1]

In my study of Greek philosophy, I learned of a group of philosophers who would mentally review their previous day in detail before getting out of bed. They did so because their group centered around reincarnation, and they were strengthening their memory. That way, they felt they would be better prepared after death to choose their next life.[2] Reincarnation aside, I have tried these strengthening exercises several times during my life, each time practicing them regularly for a couple of months. I can attest that these exercises were effective in keeping me alert to how my words and actions were affecting others.

Keep in mind that progress may be slow and that benefits will accrue over time. Most important, relax and accept that you are a human being. Loving yourself is, after all, some of what you are seeking.

2. How might general knowledge about shared death experiences affect our society as a whole?

Some speculate that if everyone knew about shared death experiences and their implications for life after death, it would spiritually transform the whole world. Love and kindness would break out like a pandemic of peace. Such a thing sounds wonderful, but personally, I doubt that the effects would be that dramatic. Why do I feel that way? Because one should be loving and kind and happy to be alive even if there isn't proof of life after death. Instead, there is increasingly less gratitude in the world, with more and more people exhibiting anger and unhappiness at the world around them. Being without proof of an afterlife should be reason to savor life, not be less happy.

In essence, I am saying that human nature likes conflict, with others and ourselves. It would take not proof of life after life but a change in human nature for a worldwide shift.

Plus, in reality, most of us have a difficult time even imagining our own death, let alone envisioning a life after it. To paraphrase Sigmund Freud, most of us believe we will be spectators to our own death, watching someone else pass as we then go on our eternal way.

3. Why do some people experience shared death experiences and others don't?

I have no idea. I do know that about 10 to 20 percent of those who recover from cardiac arrest (the gold standard of a near-death experience) report having had a near-death experience,[3] which leaves the door open to there being far more that go unreported. Perhaps underreporting is a challenge in shared death experiences (SDEs) too.

Part of the challenge is that while we know why NDEs occur, namely a resuscitation, it isn't known why SDEs occur. Being close to someone who is physically dying is of course one reason. But being in the proximity of a dying person is not always required, as is illustrated by those who have precognitive experiences where the SDE may involve someone who is dying unexpectedly at a great distance away.

There have been no studies of the frequency of SDEs. I do know from conversations with colleagues and patients that there are far more SDEs than even I would expect. If I ask attendees at a conference how many have had SDEs or know of friends or family who have, a very high percentage of hands go up.

As with NDEs, discovering that there is a name and definition for these experiences gives people a handle by which they can grasp a greater understanding of what it is that leads to having this amazing experience.

4. What is the medical significance of shared death experiences?

Very few medical doctors can address questions about near-death experiences and shared death experiences, not because they aren't interested but because their training doesn't include handling mystical questions such as those dealing with life after death. Because of that, and without a note of cynicism, it is truthful to say that questions about life after life are considered irrelevant by physicians to their clinical role.

Why should doctors need to know about SDEs? For at least two clinical reasons:

1. SDEs can be mentally and physically jolting for a patient. One who has had an SDE needs to at least be able to talk to an expert about what happened just to ventilate and get it off their chest. A doctor should be able to fulfill that function, even minimally.

2. A doctor—every doctor—needs to be able to assure those who've had shared death experiences that they are not alone. For a patient to know that what they've experienced happens to others is a great relief.

5. If medical doctors aren't prepared to talk about shared death experiences, then who is?

Whom you should talk to depends upon your needs. If you are seeking help with grief and need a cognitive approach to confront the death of a loved one, then I highly recommend consulting a psychologist. Make certain that the psychologist is trained in grief therapy and is willing and able to address your concerns even if those concerns have a metaphysical bent to them.

If you want to explore deeper and broader, a good conversation with a person trained in rational exploration, a student of philosophy, for instance, would be useful to help you confront the mysteries of the afterlife in a rational way. Some philosophers are deeply interested in questions about life after death and are willing to converse on this history, which goes back to ancient Greeks like Plato and Pythagoras. It is a thrilling course of study that delves deeply into one of mankind's most frequently asked questions: What happens when we die?

6. Where do we go from here? What does the future of research into shared death experiences and life after death look like?

I think the future of afterlife research is to remodel our minds to interact with shared death experiences in a new way. By preparing our minds in advance with study, we can more clearly and intelligibly explain near-death experiences and shared death experiences to others. Doing this preparation will bring about a veritable breakthrough in rational investigation of the afterlife.

That sounds extraordinary and incredible, I realize. However, I base that belief on sixty years of research into NDEs and SDEs, and I am fully confident I can defend my claim successfully, which is that knowledge is the key to philosophical breakthroughs.

7. What advice do you have for people who have a fear of death?

Reasonably speaking we all have a fear of death. So, I don't think it's realistic to tell someone that they shouldn't have such a fear. Instead, I tell them to study the medical literature that indicates a survival of bodily death. Talk to those who have had near-death experiences or shared death experiences. They are all around you in any setting. How do you find these people? Figure out a way to bring up the subject of NDEs or SDEs. You will be surprised and glad you did. Fear is often just a lack of knowledge. So, yes, educate yourself with the study of these phenomena through books and conversation. Don't fear education. In the end, it's your friend.

Have you had a near-death experience, a shared death experience, or a related experience that you would like to share? Do you have questions about the afterlife? Reach out to us by going to proofoflifeafterlife.com and filling out the question form.

How to Build Your Own Psychomanteum

---✳---

After reading about this procedure, many people want to try it for themselves. If you fit into that category, here are basic instructions for evoking spirits of the deceased by mirror gazing. The first thing to remember is that there is no exact formula. But a relaxed frame of mind helps facilitate experiences like this.

You will need to prepare a space in which to encounter the spirits of this deceased. Choose a room that you are able to darken by closing the door, lowering the shades, or drawing the curtains. A walk-in closet works fine. Mount a mirror on the wall high enough so that you cannot see your reflection when you sit in a comfortable chair three feet in front of the wall. A reclining chair works best, for it allows you to relax your body in a comfortable position.

The mirror needs to be large enough so that it occupies a large percentage of your visual field. Again, don't get fixated on the exact dimensions of the mirror. The one I used was four feet by four feet or so, but smaller mirrors are fine too. Put a small light bulb behind your chair, about twenty watts, so the light comes up in the room and diffusely illuminates the mirror.

You want to exclude as many reflections as you can, but to exclude them all is virtually impossible. Just go by trial and error until you find an arrangement that feels comfortable.

When you begin mirror gazing, it is best not to have an agenda at first. Just gaze into the mirror and relax. Let your mind go free and see what happens. Most see mist and clouds initially, which then may shift into formed visions. Many people say they first see scenery, mountains or forest lakes. Or they may see people interacting in complex environments such as inside a building or in a town setting. Sometimes mirror gazers hatch creative ideas. Quite a few artists over the years have told me they use mirror gazing to tap into their creativity and get ideas for paintings or writing stories.

After you become acquainted with mirror gazing without a specific agenda, you can go on to the process of evoking the deceased. Choose someone who has died whom you would like to see again. Preferably, you should ask a friend or relative you trust to assist in your journey. The assistant is there to ask you questions about your lost loved one, mainly questions you may not have thought of on your own. The idea of having a friend ask questions is to get your process of thinking and feeling started.

There are no specific time constraints in this process. The goal is to continue your interchange with your assistant until your departed loved one is vivid in your mind. Once you have accomplished this, sit in the chair before the mirror and gaze into the mirror as though you were gazing into an infinite depth.

The magic of this experience comes not from the mirror, but from your mind. Relax, get comfortable, and drift down into the feeling you have when you are on the verge of sleep, a state known as the hypnogogic state. Don't put yourself under time pressure. You might take off your watch and silence your phone, putting it away from your reach, before you begin gazing. Let the process unfold in its own tempo.

I recommend keeping a notebook to jot down your impressions following each session. Over time your will reach a visionary state quicker and more effectively as you advance in your understanding of the process.

About the Authors

---*---

Raymond A. Moody Jr., MD, PhD

MARLIN DARRAH

Raymond Moody, MD, PhD, is the leading authority on the "near-death experience"—a phrase he coined and an experience he defined in the late seventies. His seminal work, *Life After Life*, completely changed the way we view death and dying and has sold more than thirteen million copies worldwide. The *New York Times* calls Dr. Moody the "father of the near-death experience."

For more than five decades, Dr. Moody has regularly enlightened audiences with his lectures and public speaking events. His Life after Life Institute provides a place for leading-edge researchers and thinkers to share their investigations into near-death phenomena and offers online courses and personal consultations. Dr. Moody is also in the private practice of philosophical counseling and consulting on dying, training hospice workers, clergy, psychologists, nurses, doctors, and other medical professionals on matters of grief recovery and dying.

Dr. Moody received his medical degree from the College of Georgia and his PhD in philosophy from the University of Virginia where he also received his MA and BA. He is the recipient of many awards including the World Humanitarian Award and a bronze medal in the Human Relations category at the New York Film Festival for the movie version of *Life After Life*. Dr. Moody is a frequent media guest and has appeared on *The Oprah Winfrey Show* three times, as well as on hundreds of other local and nationally syndicated programs such as *Today*, *ABC's Turning Point*, and *MSNBC: Grief Recovery*.

Paul Perry

SYDNEY SHERMAN

Paul Perry is the coauthor of five *New York Times* bestsellers, including *The Light Beyond* with Raymond Moody, *Saved by the Light* with Dannion Brinkley, and *Evidence of the Afterlife* with Jeffrey Long, MD. Perry has cowritten a dozen books on near-death experiences, six of them with Dr. Moody. His books have been published in more than thirty languages around the world.

Paul is also a documentary filmmaker whose work has appeared on worldwide television. His best-known film, *Jesus: the Lost Years*, a documentary based on his book *Jesus in Egypt*, has aired more than twenty times in the United States. His most recent film, *The Secrets and Mysteries of Christopher Columbus*, has been viewed nearly four million times on the British history streaming channel, Timeline of History. For his film and book about artist Salvador Dalí, Paul was knighted in Portugal and is the official filmmaker of the Portuguese royal family.

Paul is a graduate of Arizona State University and Antioch University in Los Angeles, as well as a former fellow at the prestigious Gannett Center for Media Studies at Columbia University in New York City where he studied public health. He taught magazine writing at the University of Oregon in Eugene, Oregon, and was executive editor of *American Health* magazine, a winner of the National Magazine Awards for General Excellence. Since becoming a full-time writer, Paul has written or cowritten more than twenty books on a variety of topics, including biography, health, medical science, and history.